Adventure at High Risk

ADVENTURE AT HIGH RISK
Stories from Around the Globe

Edited by Cameron M. Burns and Kerry L. Burns

LYONS PRESS
Guilford, Connecticut
An imprint of Globe Pequot Press

To buy books in quantity for corporate use
or incentives, call **(800) 962-0973**
or e-mail **premiums@GlobePequot.com.**

Lyons Press is an imprint of Globe Pequot Press.

Acquisitions editor: David Legere
Project editor: Meredith Dias
Layout artist: Melissa Evarts

Library of Congress Cataloging-in-Publication Data is available on file.

ISBN 978-0-7627-8600-8

Printed in the United States of America

For Zoe Elizabeth Burns and Mollie Frances Burns,
members of the next generation of adventurers

CONTENTS

Acknowledgments

Thanks to the many members of the clan who read initial drafts of this book, including Mary, Gillian, Penny, Ann, Michael, Jan, Peter, and Sue Burns; Pat Webb; Rob, Kian, and Gill Murdoch; Heather and Rod Gough; and Bob and Sylvia Robertson.

Many folks from the outdoor community helped us find the authors we wanted and their stories, including Luke and Mel Laeser; Amory and Judy Lovins; Steve and Sandi Porcella; Mike and Claire Schillaci; Ted, Amber, and Jesse Davenport; John and Laurel Catto; Benny Bach; Jordan Campbell; Rick Leonidas; Charlie French; Julian Fisher; Trip Hyde; Chad Riley; Doug Leen; Todd Gordon; Jacob Schmitz; Misha Logvinov; Andrea Peacock; Ellen Brennan; Joe and Nancy McKeown; Chris Lomax; Ethan Putterman; Allen Hill; Karen Gilbert; Leslie Henderson; Stephen Venables; Paul Ross; Chris Bonington; and.... Thank you. Thanks also to the staff of Mesa Public Library, Los Alamos, and especially to Ruth McKee, the interlibrary loan librarian.

The staff at Globe Pequot was also very helpful—and, more importantly, patient—when it came to the never-ending dance of W-9s, W-8s, and permission releases. Thank you, David Legere (seriously, Dave, this was a massive headache), Meredith Dias, Elissa Curcio, Steve Culpepper, and (former GPer) Jess Haberman. Thanks also to Sarah Warner of Warner Literary Group for keeping us on task.

Finally, thank you Zoe and Mollie Burns, for keeping the adventure flame burning. We've already climbed, skied, sailed, backpacked, surfed, snowboarded, horsepacked, rafted, paddleboarded, canoed, and spelunked in your respective thirteen and eleven years—let's do it lots more.

INTRODUCTION

WHAT MAKES A GOOD ADVENTURE STORY? WE PONDERED THAT question when compiling this selection of stories. Does a good adventure story involve risk? Certainly there's risk in just about everything that we do, so maybe. Does it involve unknown geography? It might, but then again, it might not—some of the best adventures occur within a few miles of home. Adversity? Maybe, maybe not.

And, early in the evolution of this book, we realized that true adventure isn't as much about the objective as it is about the idea of adventure, and what these writers were willing to try. After deep consideration, we realized that good adventure stories aren't relegated to just time, place, adversity, and risk—among other factors. Rather, good adventure stories come from genuine thinkers—individuals who get themselves out there and not only take it all in, but share, retell, and posit the real, the imaginary, the possible, and the impossible.

Thinkers like the true Class-A adventurers whose stories appear in this collection. Thinkers like Stephen Venables, who in 1988 made the first ascent of the Kangshung Face of Everest, a remarkable achievement by any measure. Stephen, by our definition (and arguably the general public's opinion, as the Kangshung Face made him world famous in the mountaineering community) is a true adventurer. In this collection, we don't have a story about his Everest adventure; instead we include a fascinating piece Stephen wrote about a remarkably ambitious and engaging low-key expedition to Patagonia ("Monte Sarmiento").

In 1977 Robyn Davidson traveled 1,700 miles—solo and on foot—from Alice Springs to the Indian Ocean, across the harshest country Australia has to offer. Her subsequent book

Tracks (1978) was a worldwide bestseller, and her trek across the Outback became Australia's best-known adventure story of the period. Here we include a fairly straightforward story by Robyn about traveling the United States on a Harley—this is a massively different adventure from *Tracks*, and her take on modern America is much more interesting than her observations about camels.

Good adventure stories include reflection on both the part of the author and the part of the reader. Genuine adventurers think differently, and when they look back at what they've done, it's often some of the best reflection one can read. The people who wrote these stories weren't wondering *if* they could get something done; they were wondering *how* they'd get it done.

That said, while many of the stories included here offer a great deal of reflection, some are quite short on reflection—meaning it's we the readers who need to ponder what's going on. Chris Davenport's story ("Pyramid Peak, East Face") about skiing the sheer east side of Pyramid Peak in the Colorado Rockies is one such piece, as it's only 511 words. But put in the context of what Chris achieved that winter, the story becomes a window into his amazing world, a world of cutting-edge descents all over the planet to the point where he hardly has time to sit down, let alone write a philosophical treatise on what he's up to.

The same is true for Christina Dodwell's horseback adventures in Eastern Turkey ("Bandit Border & Noah Was Here"). When we started reading those pieces, we thought it was good storytelling, but as they went on it became evident that this was one independent, determined, and truly tough woman. (Having rocks thrown at her while she's riding through various villages in the absolute middle of nowhere? Seriously?)

In all, this collection is a truly eclectic mix—as an *adventure* collection should be. It's got BASE jumping and rock climbing, skiing and spelunking, horseback exploration and motorcycle travels, kayaking and cycling. But the thread that ties them together is that they are stories by Class-A adventurers who came back, thought deeply about what they'd done, and shared their journeys—the trials, the strangeness, the dirt, and the beauty.

We hope you enjoy all of them.

—Cameron M. Burns, Kerry L. Burns
May 2014

BASE

Matt Gerdes

Editors' note: Matt Gerdes is the author of The Great Book of BASE *(www.base-book.com), widely considered to be the premier reference for the intrepid participants in this fast-growing but always-fringe sport. He has completed over a thousand safe BASE jumps to date, the vast majority of them being wingsuit flights from alpine cliffs. He is an avid backcountry skier, surfer, and climber, residing in the French Alps and the Pacific Northwest. Matt is also the founder of Squirrel (www .squirrel.ws), a leading wingsuit and BASE equipment manufacturer.*

Standing on the ridge, screaming into a slashing arctic wind, I scream to Jimmy. "Hurry the fuck up!" I'm freezing, shivering, trembling and hunched over. I'm waiting to video his jump, and I have no idea that these are the last words that I will ever speak to my friend, or that I am about to watch him die.

For me, in a way, it all started with the Eiger . . . and with Jimmy. We were paragliding in the French Alps back when Jimmy was a new BASE jumper and I barely knew what the sport really was. It was a cold and humid day in May with just a bit too much wind for flying, so we were lolling around in the grass at St Vincent Les Forts. I was watching him pack his BASE canopy. He looked up at me, excited, and told me that he was going to BASE jump the North Face of the Eiger in August. I was stunned. "Is that even possible?" I asked. Yeah, it gets jumped quite a bit, you just have to walk up there. My astonishment rapidly morphed into excited determination. "Can I come?" I asked.

"Sure," he said, "but you have to learn to BASE jump first."

Five days later I was sitting in a Pilatus Porter, climbing to altitude over Gap-Tallard, France. I only had a few days in Gap-Tallard with my instructor, a calm and level-headed Englishman by the name of Kevin Hardwick, in which time I completed 11 skydives, which was about 200 skydives less than the generally accepted minimum to begin BASE jumping. But, I figured, with 1000 hours flying paragliders and my superhuman outdoor sports skills, I'd be fine. I was young, and foolish.

Skydivers, for all their long-haired left-leaning yahoo-screaming tendencies, are a dogmatic and hierarchical group. They set rules and, for the most part, live by them and enforce them upon each other. Experience and capability in skydiving is often defined with jump numbers, and a skydiver with 500 jumps will normally be considered better than a skydiver with 300 jumps, even though the opposite is often true depending on the person. If the rulebooks states that one needs "X" number of jumps to try a new skill, then there is usually someone inspecting your logbook when you want to try it. If you have a question or a problem, you refer to someone with more jump numbers than you.

Most BASE jumpers are experienced skydivers first, and traditionally skydivers were not allowed to even think about BASE jumping until they had years in the sport and hundreds of sky-dives. The subtleties of canopy flight for landing, and body flight in freefall, require much time to master. Thus, with just 11 skydives and virtually no time at all in the sport, I was seriously breaking the rules by planning to BASE jump. Fortunately for me, I knew people. A good friend referred me to his good friend, Greg Nevelo, who was willing to not only teach someone with so little experience, but take time out of his schedule to drive 17 hours with me to the Perrine Bridge in Idaho, where BASE jumping is legal and accepted. The Perrine Bridge spans a gorge through which the slow-moving Snake River meanders, 150m below. It's not a huge jump by any means, but the legality, ease of access, a nice landing zone on the riverbank, and the water itself all make it an ideal place to learn the basics of BASE jumping. Although hitting the water at 150km/h will be the fatal result of failing to deploy a parachute, the water does provide a certain amount of protection against canopy malfunctions and late deployments, if they occur. The Perrine Bridge now sees more first jumps than any other object in the world and is generally considered one of the safest jumps on earth, yet five jumpers have died there in the past 10 years.

As I climbed over the railing and looked down to the green water below, I was filled with 60% fear, 30% excitement, and 10% "what-the-fuck-am-I-doing" doubt. Officially, I should have been skydiving for at least a few months, if not a few years, and I should have had over 200 skydives already under my belt. But I was committed. Greg was calm, and I could almost hear his instructions over the sound of my pulse. My mouth was dry, and my hands were wet. Knowing that I wouldn't become less scared by standing there, I left the bridge, fell into the dead windless air, and time ground to a halt.

A falling body accelerates from 0–100km/h in just 3 seconds. At about 10 seconds, acceleration levels off and we're hurtling toward the earth at almost 200km/h. It is a curious fact that although during this acceleration physical time is generally static, mental time can be elastic. Stepping into space, hundreds of meters over the ground, time bends. A minute's worth of thoughts pass through your head in the first millisecond, but at the same time you are so focused on only this, only the jump, that you're thinking of nothing. It is a level of focus that could be compared to a Zen master in deep meditation, and all you need to do to achieve it is commit suicide with a plan B. My mind races, constantly, in a ceaseless internal dialogue that has plagued me since pre-adolescence. I have only ever found solace while in situations of agitated excitement; states of mind that came most easily while rock climbing, backcountry skiing, or whitewater kayaking. While I'm doing something that requires my full attention in order to prevent serious injury or death, my mind is at ease. And BASE, I realized instantly, was the ultimate in neurological satisfaction.

As my feet stepped into nothing and my mind relaxed into intense focus, I wondered what was taking so long for my parachute to open. That second felt like a half-minute, and as my parachute banged open and the opening forced my chin to my chest and my gaze downward, I realized that I had fallen barely 50m and now had over 100m remaining to steer my parachute to landing. I touched down in the field and instead of feeling like I had just accomplished something I was overwhelmed with a sense of having taken just one small step of a long and serious journey. I made seven jumps at the Perrine Bridge over a couple of days, and then got back on a plane to the Alps. I had Eiger fever.

When I arrived back in Europe, I headed for Austria. I had 11 skydives and 7 BASE jumps. It was now the beginning of July, about six weeks after Jimmy had told me to get busy, and I felt like I was already behind schedule. I had less than two months to get ready to jump the Eiger, so I immediately started conning my paraglider friends into letting me jump out of their tandem wings. Mike Schoenherr, a Zillertal local and experienced BASE jumper, took me to the Euro Bridge and gave me a few pointers. I had known him for years but we were to become closer through the sport of BASE over time, until BASE took him from us all in 2008. Over the next few weeks, with the help of my friends, I racked up a few more BASE jumps and even went back to France to make a handful of skydives. Before I knew it, August had arrived and I was standing on the edge of my first cliff.

It is commonly said that, on a long enough timeline, BASE is guaranteed fatal. This is because in order to survive a BASE jump, everything has to work out 100% OK. I don't mean that you have to do everything 100% right, or that every aspect of the situation needs to be 100% perfect. I mean that, when all is said and done, things need to work out. Luck has saved countless jumpers, simple stupid strokes of luck. The best way to maximize luck's effectiveness is to do things right. If you operate at a 98% rate of perfection, then you'll only need luck 2% of the time. If you operate at 80%, then you're asking a lot of your schutzengel—probably too much.

Overwhelmingly, the vast majority of BASE deaths have occurred at cliff objects. Whether or not the vast majority of BASE jumps occur from cliffs is difficult to say, but the statistics (more than 60% of all fatalities since 1981 have occurred at cliffs) do suggest that cliffs are by far the most deadly of objects. Perhaps this is because BASE jumpers are drawn to the aura and mystique of alpine cliffs before they have had adequate proper training at a bridge, or maybe it is because of the varied and technical terrain that most cliffs present us with—either way, I'm glad I didn't know that when I was standing at the top of my first cliff jump, technically unprepared and wholly scared.

I was with my friend Jimmy, of course. I had been ever since I decided to begin BASE jumping, even when he was 6,000 miles away at his home in Hawaii while I was practicing paraglider jumps in the Alps—every step I made, I reported back, eager to convince him that I'd be ready to hang out with him and his friend Gray during the upcoming Eiger trip. And here we were, Jimmy, Gray, and I, standing at the top of a 400m limestone cliff in Switzerland, the Eiger looming out of sight a few kilometers behind us. The cliff we stood upon was only the beginning; this was the kid's stuff. But I knew I was already in over my head. I thought to myself that this needed to go well in order for me to be ready for the Eiger in a couple of weeks. I then thought, "going well" meant surviving, uninjured. It was a sobering realization. I knew that I could trip on exit, and tumble out of control. I could jump into a too "head-down" position, and either end up on my back, or in somersaulting instability, unable to deploy my parachute correctly. Or, everything could go entirely well until my parachute opened, facing the cliff, giving me less than a second to turn it 180 degrees or slam into the wall, tumbling to the talus below. Maybe my parachute would open on heading, facing away from the wall, but with a knot or tangle in the lines, putting me into an uncontrollable spiraling turn, which I would ride all the way into the trees. Or maybe I just wouldn't find my pilot chute in time, and would impact the forest below with no parachute out at all.

The myriad ways that I could die right then swarmed through my brain. I understood the risks, and I knew what I needed to do right then to avoid them. I knew what I had done already to avoid them as well: I had packed my parachute as cleanly as possible, hopefully cleanly enough to allow a nice deployment with no line entanglements or other malfunctions. I had jumped successfully from other objects—bridges and paragliders—with no stability problems. And I knew how to "track"—how to fly my body away from the cliff in freefall—poorly, at least. I needed to pull my minimal experience together, and focus. Standing there, looking into the valley below with Jimmy and Gray just behind me, I saw myself taking a powerful step off of the edge. I imagined leaning forward just enough for a good tracking position, and I visualized myself flying my body away from the cliff and opening my parachute facing away from the wall and then landing it gently in the grassy field below. In my mind, it went perfectly.

Fear can be energizing, or paralyzing. If one can turn fear into energy, and use it to stimulate mind and body, it becomes a powerful ally for the sport of BASE jumping. In contrast, if fear leads to mental and physical paralysis or even delayed reactions, you will die. My heart was pounding in my chest, blood throbbing against my eardrums. I could almost hear the sound of my pulse drumming against my jacket, and my heartbeat seemed to shake my eyeballs in their sockets.

Although I felt like the fear I was experiencing was pushing me to the limits of paralysis, as I took a deep breath and leapt forward I felt tense and powerful. I leaned into a decent track and moved away from the wall a little bit before opening my parachute, well above the trees and on-heading. Even before I landed, I knew that my first cliff jump was a success, and I was desperately eager to do it again, and again. I knew then that I wanted the Eiger to be only the first chapter of a longer story.

Three weeks later, I had around 30 BASE jumps, and although I was still a nervous beginner I had reached an acceptable level of comfort and was no longer shitting stale Twinkies before each jump. And the Eiger was coming into season. Less snow covered the west face, and the "Pilz," a pillar of rock that stood off the west ridge, was largely free of ice. Over the past few weeks, while I had been overwhelmed by learning the basics of the sport, Jimmy was moving up to the next step: wingsuiting. Coached by our vastly more experienced friend, Gray Fowler, Jimmy had made his first wingsuit jumps and was ready to fly the Eiger with Gray. I was in awe of Jimmy and Gray, and although I knew I wanted to wingsuit one day as well, that day felt far away due to the amount of skydive training that I lacked. I would need to make hundreds more skydives in order to fly a wingsuit safely from a cliff, and I didn't even have 20 jumps from an airplane yet. Not to mention the fact that jumping the Eiger without a wingsuit was really all the excitement I could possibly stand. The thought of complicating such an intimidating jump was absolutely unbearable at the time. But Jimmy was feeling pretty good about it, and Gray was, as always, his cool and reserved self. A native of Texas, Gray spoke softly but in a steady and solid tone. His soothing and knowledgeable voice had been a constant in the background of my first 30 jumps, and Jimmy's entire wingsuit BASE training had depended on it as well. Gray was our "mother hen," and we trusted him completely. He had already wingsuited the Eiger the year before, and it was him who we followed on our path to the Pilz.

The Eiger is a special mountain, and not only because its reputation necessarily precedes it. Its dark northern face sits so high over the horizon that it seems half of Europe must cringe under its gaze. A dirty mess of crumbling rock varying in tones from light grey to coal black, the North Face and summit are capped perennially in white strands of snow, intensifying the darkness of the rock. Even in late August as we stood on the Pilz with the North Face stretched out to our right, the upper half was 60% covered in freshly fallen snow. And it was cold. At 3000m, we shivered and geared up, glancing frequently down the face. Jimmy and Gray were wearing their wings and talking about where they would fly to. I was focusing on a good track and a safe opening; while the Eiger is steep below the Pilz for almost 400m, after that it becomes quickly positive and a series of ledges step out and turn into a long talus slope. A rock dropped from the Pilz will impact the ledges below after about 8 seconds, and I was hoping to track away from the wall for closer to 20 seconds.

Jimmy and Gray jumped first, together. They flew away from the face, toward Grindelwald in the valley far below. Jimmy pulled after less than 20 seconds, overwhelmed by the intensity of the experience and just happy to be far away from the wall while still very high. Gray set a course for the valley, and flew for 57 seconds before opening his parachute over the Alpiglen train station. At the time, it was one of the coolest things I had ever seen in my life. A 57 second BASE jump! I was blown away. But I was jarred back to reality when I realized it was my turn. I wasted little time, wanting to get it over with, and jumped. Immediately after leaving the Pilz, the ledges I couldn't see while standing on exit became apparent. They were still almost 400m away, but the steepness of the slope in the cool shadows of the northern face made it hard to tell the difference between 100m and 500m. I was making progress forward, but my point of impact was still one of those ledges . . . how far were they . . . questions raced through my head in a series of sensations and unconscious calculations, not verbal thoughts. Suddenly very scared, I decided to pull, even though I felt like I might be far enough away to clear the next series of steps in the wall. When my parachute opened, facing the rock, I realized how wrong I had been. My hands darted up to my brakes and I thrust the right handle down to my waist, turning my parachute away from a snowy ledge with less than 2m to spare. I looked down the wall, now flying away from it, and realized that I had just come closer to death than I had been in any other moment of my life. If I had waited a fraction of a second longer in freefall, or had reacted a fraction of a second slower in turning my parachute, I'd be a stain on the limestone talus below. I felt very small, and very lucky. I knew that I had just gotten away with something, and that I might never be so lucky again—I needed to train properly to survive in this sport.

And train I did. I went skydiving again, and moved to the south of France, where my new home was less than an hour from the Gorges du Verdon. There, I could repeat multiple cliff jumps per day, as the exit points were just meters from the road and an easy trail led out of the gorge back to where my car would be parked. I dove into action, and racked up jump numbers there. I honed my landing skills in the tiny landing areas that were nestled between the oak trees and limestone boulders in the bottom of the gorge, and my packing became faster and cleaner. I also returned to Switzerland frequently to practice tracking from slightly larger cliffs. Although Jimmy lived on the other side of the world in Hawaii, he and I stayed in constant communication, always planning our next BASE adventure. We did another month in Switzerland together the following summer of 2005, and then late in 2006 I traveled to Hawaii to train myself to fly a wingsuit with him, at the skydive center near his home. Our plan was to fly wingsuits together the following spring of 2007, on Baffin Island.

Through a friend in the BASE world, I had been offered the opportunity to travel to Baffin Island on a private expedition led by BASE jumpers from California. I instantly accepted, committing to the trip, and then called Jimmy to tell him the news. He was even more excited than I was to hear that an expedition was going, and he was instantly desperate to get onboard. I told him that I would do my best to convince the expedition leaders, and he resolved to convince his life and work partner, Stefanie, that he should be able to take three weeks out of their busy life in order to travel north of the Arctic Circle and then jump from the world's largest sheer granite faces. Jimmy figured that it would be easy, and when I was with him at his home in Hawaii for the wingsuit training, we put it simply to Stefanie: "Baffin is safe! The cliffs are so big, and so steep, that it's practically like skydiving, and just as safe! Don't worry, it will be fine."

"If you die, I am going to be SO MAD at you!" She said, half-joking.

My wingsuit training started poorly. I had less than 40 skydives, when I should have had 200 in order to jump the wingsuit I was using. I figured that I was a talented young athlete and the rules that applied to average people could be bent for me, but as I tumbled out of control 3km above the north shore of Oahu and then struggled to fly the suit in a straight line, I began to have second thoughts. After a couple of days of stress and doubt, I finally managed to fly in a straight line and make some half-controlled turns but I realized I was far from being ready to BASE jump a wingsuit. Looking back, I realize now that I wasn't taking the sport seriously enough. I hadn't experienced or witnessed any real consequences and the severity and finality of a BASE jumping mistake was still only theoretically bad in my mind. Soon, that would change.

The Baffin trip was scheduled shortly after an event for my work in the Canary Islands. Part of my job as Marketing Manager for Ozone Paragliders was to travel to paragliding events and put on air shows with "The Ozone Team," an aerial demonstration team of my own creation. On this trip, I had invited a friend and fellow BASE jumper with years more experience than me, and a reputation as one of the best wingsuit pilots in the world. Stefan Oberlander was a friend of Gray's, and I was hoping that he would not only add to our demo team show, but also be able to teach me a thing or two about wingsuit BASE jumping. Stefan and I got along pretty well, and had already shared some excellent adventures skiing and speed flying together in the Alps. But the adventure in El Hierro would be our last.

Midway through our trip, Stefan planned to jump out of a paraglider with his wingsuit and then fly very close to the top of a hill above the normal landing area. He was well adept at flying close to terrain, and no one thought twice about his intended flight path. I had just landed a speed flying wing at the bottom of the hill with my friend Mike, when we both heard what sounded like a cross between a canopy opening and a car crash. I looked up and saw our friend who was flying the paraglider Stefan jumped from in a spiraling descent, headed to a point just above us on the hill. In an instant, I knew exactly what had happened. While approaching the hill, he had realized that his flight path was too low to clear the top of it. Too late, he deployed his parachute as he crashed into the dry brush on the hillside. When we reached him moments later, he was alive but losing consciousness. We did our best to stabilize him for the evacuation but his injuries were internal. A helicopter came and flew him to a hospital that was too poorly equipped to perform the internal surgery he needed, and Stefan died in the second helicopter that was meant to take him to a bigger hospital.

I had known that it was bound to happen, sooner or later. I had expected that someone I knew would eventually die BASE jumping, but I had been half expecting that person to be me. Certainly not Stefan—not someone good, not someone experienced, not someone with good judgment and a solid reputation for being responsible—he was one of the people who didn't have accidents, one of the people who didn't make judgment errors.

When I met Jimmy in Ottawa on our way to north to Baffin, I told him the story. Jimmy also thought that Stefan was not the type of person who dies BASE jumping. He was too calculating, too experienced. I had a newfound respect for wingsuiting, so when Jimmy asked me if I brought my wingsuit, I said yes. What I didn't say was that I already knew I wouldn't be jumping it on Baffin. I had enough to think about already.

High above the permafrost of Northern Canada, we were giddy on the last flight from Iqaluit to Clyde River. Our team of 12 jumpers contained 11 Baffin rookies; only the team leader had been there before. For Jimmy, it was the fulfillment of a dream of many years and, he felt, the pinnacle of his BASE career. Already immersed in a full time shark diving venture in Hawaii, Jimmy had been offered a major television role as the host of Discovery Channel's "Shark Week," and he felt that his life was returning to a focus on the ocean. Mountain sports, like BASE jumping, were about to become a part of his past and for him, this was his last BASE hurrah. I had no intention of stopping my BASE career after Baffin, but the thought of not having Jimmy as a jump partner made me feel lonely and insecure. My entry to the sport and each step through it so far had been accomplished either at his side, or with plans to be there. Jimmy threw himself into our Arctic adventure like it was the last time he'd be anywhere amazing, and the first time he'd seen anything so interesting. He had climbed 6000m peaks in the Andes and flown his paraglider from the summits, sailed a tiny boat cross the Pacific Ocean multiple times, lived in places with names like Guam and Vanuatu, and run from the exploding debris of live volcanoes. He had petted a great white shark while swimming outside the cage with it, surfed 10m waves, and generally lived through more in the first 40 years of his life than most men could in five lifetimes, yet every little experience on Baffin Island seemed to impress him more than anyone else on the team. Jimmy, simply put, just got more out of his life, every minute.

Base camp tended to revolve around Jimmy's stories when he was in the main tent. I followed him everywhere and we decided together when and what to jump. He was wingsuiting, and I was still only "tracking" so although we could often jump from the same exit points, Jimmy soon chose one that was too deep in a canyon for me to track out. It was a "wingsuit only" kind of jump. When Jimmy hiked up for that one, I still went, of course. My plan was to jump another point on the front of the wall, so Jimmy gave me one of his video cameras and asked me to film from the opposite side of the canyon while he jumped with two of our friends. They planned to do a "three-way," meaning that all three of them would exit at the same time, and then fly out of the canyon together, Jimmy bringing up the rear and filming them with the camera mounted to his helmet.

And so there I stood, shivering uncontrollably, facing into an Arctic wind. It had taken them some time to put on their wingsuits; with large snow boots, insulated clothing, and stiff limbs from the cold, everything took more time. I yelled Jimmy's name . . . "Jimmy!" ". . . Freeeezzzing!" "Hurry the fuck up!"

The cold wind beat back my yelling, and I knew they couldn't hear me. I could see that they were getting ready to jump, stretching the fabric of their wingsuits to test that they were connected to their parachutes and fitted properly over their boots. They shuffled to the edge, close to each other and all three looking into the void below. Then they jumped.

Through the video camera lens, I could see three figures freefalling, accelerating quickly, and then two figures turning their fall into flight. They converted their vertical speed to horizontal flight, and started to race out of the canyon. A third figure stalled his wingsuit, with not enough of a forward angle to fly efficiently. Subconsciously, I knew it was Jimmy, but as I watched him get lower and lower in the canyon I didn't want to admit it to myself and I said, out loud, "Someone needs to pull." I changed my view from squinting through the camera lens to both eyes open, and watched as Jimmy threw his pilot chute just a few meters over the bottom of the canyon. As his parachute started to come out of his container, he impacted head first.

The sound reached me a second later. A deafening crack echoed out of the canyon, knocking me to my knees. I switched off the camera, knelt in the snow, and screamed without knowing it.

After Baffin, BASE slowed down for me, in a way. I jumped less frequently, but when I did jump it was with a sort of ferocious drive that bordered on the suicidal. I opened lower and packed faster than ever before. And I became really picky about who I jumped with. I stopped bothering to contact anyone around my home in France, and only jumped when my closest friends came over from the US to visit Europe. I chose my partners more carefully, and was drawn to a certain type of BASE jumper—the type that has been around for a while.

I looked up to a couple of friends who had been BASE jumping for 20 years and had thousands of BASE jumps. In reality, Andy West and Dave Barlia were truly excellent guys and I enjoyed their company for that reason alone, but I think subconsciously I was drawn to them because they'd been keeping themselves safe for so long that I thought I probably wouldn't have to watch them die BASE jumping. I also trusted that they wouldn't be inclined to put me into a situation that would be pushing their own limits, which were beyond mine. With them, I centered my jumping a bit, and tried to become more conservative.

Dave and Andy were wingsuit jumpers, almost exclusively. I had been planning to jump my wingsuit on Baffin with Jimmy, but Stefan's death put me off the idea of an accelerated approach to wingsuiting. Jimmy's death only made me more hesitant, but I knew I had to do it, and after returning to France for a lengthy bout of wingsuit skydiving during the summer after Baffin I knew that I was running out of excuses. I had reached that phase of my BASE career, and needed to man-up and commit.

I made my first jumps in Italy, with my Austrian friend Mike Schoenherr, who two years before had been coaching me during some of my first jumps. By then, I had over 200 normal BASE jumps and around 100 skydives, most of them being wingsuit skydives, and the transition to wingsuit BASE came easily. After a few jumps with Andy and Dave in Switzerland, I was completely hooked. I knew that from then on, I would be a wingsuit BASE jumper.

As the sport of wingsuiting has progressed, a transition has occurred. In the beginning, wingsuit pilots rejoiced in the distance that our suits allowed us to separate from the wall, the wall being the only thing that tends to frequently hurt us. Distance was the quest, and the farther we flew the better we felt. Inevitably, times change. As suits became more maneuverable and pilots honed their skills, we realized that if we could buzz within a meter of a cloud while skydiving, then we could get an even more powerful rush from skimming along the terrain during a BASE jump. Soon, the pinnacle of wingsuiting wasn't gliding far from, but racing close to, the cliff. I watched the trend with a wary eye, and progressed slowly until I ended up with a next generation wingsuit—a giant advanced suit with a leg wing that extended below my pointed toes, and arm wings that extended from wrist to ankle in an almost unbroken line. With that suit, I had power and range, and instantly I felt the pull of the cliff. In Norway, I tested the new suit by passing below the level of the road at Bispen, one of the most classic and well televised wingsuit jumps in the world. I traversed the Troll Wall, streaking past granite towers and mossy slabs, and I became totally addicted to the sensation of flying at high speed near terrain. It was like a drug, perhaps . . . but to be honest I've never experienced a drug that was this good.

After Norway, although I was hooked on speed, I still craved distance and long glides as well. It was right around then that I started spending more time with Dean Potter. BASE has captured the imaginations and lives of thousands of people, many of them from other mountain sports, and often from climbing. I had first heard Dean Potter's name when I was an adolescent novice climber passing the time between ski seasons on the rock. I never dreamed that, 15 years later and together with Dean, I would be jumping off of huge alpine cliffs wearing ridiculous nylon squirrel suits that would allow us to fly further than any human ever had before, from a new BASE jump that no one imagined existed.

In the 1960s and '70s, climbing was in its golden age. Unclimbed peaks abounded, and technology and technique were advancing at yet unseen rates. Masters of alpinism and big wall climbing were finding and establishing classic routes, plucking them from the world's mountains and cliffs like low hanging fruit. For the past five years, wingsuiting has been in its golden age, and we probably have several more years of mind blowing advances to enjoy. Wingsuits have increased in size, efficiency, and usability, and normal BASE exit points that were previously deemed unjumpable or uninteresting have now become world class wingsuit jumps.

Over the past five years, countless amazing new wingsuit cliffs have been opened. Without a wingsuit, a BASE jumper can expect to enjoy a nice 7 to 9 second freefall from an average 350–400m cliff, which is a common and abundant size of cliff in the Alps. Frequently, there is a talus slope beneath that cliff, and with a wingsuit we can out-fly the talus, greatly increasing the usable altitude of the jump. For instance, in the French Alps near Grenoble, the Dent de Crolles juts out of the Massif des Vercours, a region long famous for climbing. The Dent de Crolles is a 350m limestone nipple that extends above a large treed talus slope that becomes the plateau de St Hilaire. 1km from the cliff, and at the edge of the plateau, another cliff drops away to the Rhone Valley, about 1800m below the summit of "The Dent." Although the Dent itself is only a 7 second, 350m BASE jump without a wingsuit, once we put our wings on it becomes an 1800m, 2 minute BASE flight, and that changes everything. Exit points like this all over the world can now be evaluated with "wingsuit eyes," and BASE jumpers now look for "lines of flight" that were totally unimaginable just a few years before.

Dean Potter has a knack for seeing those lines and possibilities where other people do not. In fact, that could be a bit of an understatement; I should say that Dean sees the entire world differently, and seems to exist on the other side of some inspired lens, which filters out the vast majority of the material detritus that 99% of humans are obsessed with acquiring. Dean's priorities, and in fact his very essence, are perfectly aligned to catapult someone to the top of a sport such as wingsuit BASE jumping. He cares for almost nothing other than achieving summits in great style, and descending from them with the greatest possible flair. Even physically, he is gifted; at 196cm in height and with size 49 shoes, Dean's wingspan casts a formidable shadow on the ground below.

In the summer of 2009, Dean was distracted even more than usual from his climbing career by thoughts of human flight. He arrived in the Lauterbrunnen Valley of central Switzerland, where jumpers have been holing up for more than 10 years, and set his sights on the Eiger. Not one to mess around with average endeavors of any sort, Dean decided that if the "Pilz" is the biggest possible wingsuit jump in the world, then it was as good a place as any to focus his attentions on. Like some sort of skittish Yeti, Dean walks in the mountains at a pace that normal men would need to be running to match, and Dean was regularly climbing from the

Eigergletscher train station to the Pilz exit point in little more than an hour, almost twice the speed that a normal "fast" climber can do it. In July, Dean became the first person to take full advantage of the altitude that the Pilz makes available by flying all the way to the bottom of the valley. From the exit point to the flat terrain in the valley floor at Grindelwald, the vertical is over 2000m, and the flight is a little more than 5km long. Requiring a glide ratio of nearly 3:1, meaning that for every 1m you fall, you must fly forward 3m, the Pilz to Grindelwald flight had been dreamed about for 10 years but never achieved until then, and at the end of September, I became the second person to fly to the flat section of the valley floor.

Dean lives unfettered by preconceived notions of possibility. Without worrying about the fact that no one had ever flown to Grindelwald, he flew there. Another popular jump in the low valley had never seen a wingsuit pass a certain point, and without thinking about that fact, Dean passed it. When he did, I realized that the reason I hadn't flown that far was simply because I didn't think anyone could—and when he told me, I almost didn't believe him . . . but after a few tries, I caught up with him. I saw that even more important than Dean's skill as a climber and a wingsuit pilot was his ability to visualize new possibilities and his energy to realize them, without being constrained by conventional "wisdom."

In late August, Dean began his search for a bigger jump. His theory was that the Eiger was a big mountain, and although the spindly overhanging Pilz was a special geographic figure unlike much of the North Face, there must be another exit point higher on the peak. As for the fact that no other BASE jumper had found a higher exit in the past decade of Eiger jumping, Dean cared not. So he began his search, climbing above the Pilz and making his way slowly up the west ridge.

Dean found not one new exit point, but three. And, together with our friend Andy West, Dean discovered what is now the largest BASE jump in the world: a tiny finger of rock jutting out of the west ridge, just 300m below the very summit of the mountain. "The Ecstasy Board," as Dean named it, is a full 500m higher than the Pilz and opens up vast new possibilities for wingsuits. If you were to drop a rock from this point, it would impact the icy north face after only 5 or 6 seconds, depending on how much forward thrust you sent it with, meaning that without a wingsuit this jump is either very dangerous or very uninteresting, or both. In September 2009, I found myself standing at this new Mecca with Andy West, who was at that time the only other person to have jumped it besides Dean. The weather was clear and calm but brutally cold and I was shivering violently as we put on our suits. Andy seemed less bothered about the cold, and more concerned with the thin veneer of ice that coated the rotten limestone rock that we needed to jump from. I passed my hand over it, feeling the soft smooth glaze that, although barely visible, was terrifyingly treacherous. It would not be possible to simply fall off and live— it was mandatory to push off with our feet and jump out, away from the cliff, in order to not smash into the ledges just below. And, wearing a bulky nylon wingsuit which limited our range of motion and covered our shoes in leather booties, jumping off of a shoulder-width ice coated finger of rock at 3600m was a daunting prospect, at best.

Andy went first, and shuffled his feet slowly toward the edge, moving barely centimeters at a time on the icy precipice. He took deep breaths, exhaled forcefully, counted down, and exploded forward with surprising force. He fell for less than 3 seconds before his wingsuit began to create enough lift to sustain significant forward movement. At 5 seconds Andy was already heading for Grindelwald at over 100km/h, and it was my turn to go. Not willing to wait for more than 2 minutes until Andy reached his destination in the middle of the valley, I turned my attention to my own feet and the treacherous ice. The suede leather covering my shoes was really not the ideal material, and I doubted that anyone besides Dean and Andy and I had ever stood on ice this high in the Alps wearing the equivalent of leather moccasins. Once established on the edge, my toes hanging over the yawning north wall, I took a moment to breathe in my surroundings. It was absolutely silent— one of those perfect autumn days with barely a puff of wind until 4000m, and there wasn't another human being anywhere near me. It was the kind of quiet that you have to travel far to experience, and that can only be felt in an otherwise lifeless place. I could see so far north that I imagined the smokestacks of the Ruhrgebiet poking through the haze. The entire north face was visible, at my vantage point I could see from the talus to the summit, from East Ridge to West, and not a speck of it was exposed to sunlight; it was truly a cold, dark wall. I leaned forward, lunged from the icy finger of rock, and as always, time stopped.

Every second of a BASE jump is intense, but it is the first few moments that, for me, are the most mythically elastic. Time stretched, and a fraction of a second after my toes had left the Eiger, my view of the entire face, and seemingly all of Northern Europe, expanded from my new airborne vantage point in total quietude. Imagine hovering silently just near the summit of a massive peak, with a near vertical 3000m wall beside you. Not in the rattling chaos of a helicopter, not sitting in the seat of a paraglider harness, not attached or connected to any rope—I mean hovering freely, arms outstretched, ready to catch the wind. This, the feeling of true human flight, is our holy quest. Time slows to a near standstill, seconds extend into periods of deep focus, and the BASE jump has begun. And then suddenly, the acceleration comes. Snow covered ledges raced up at my face, coming closer and closer, and I saw my point of impact less than a second below me on the wall. But the snowy ledge that would be my death was not, because I had wings, and I swooped away into the sky and the steep face fell away from me as I glided into the valley. Grindelwald was 5km ahead of me, nestled in the valley floor. The trees were so far below that they were almost individually indistinguishable, and I could see only patches of forest interrupted by the frosty fields of late September. I was flying, higher than I ever had been on a BASE jump. It was a relaxing, fulfilling feeling, a feeling that I have never experienced in any other part of life.

People ask us why we jump all of the time, but few BASE jumpers lose sleep over this mostly unanswerable question. For me, the purest form of human flight is the ultimate, and if the price to pay for it is death, then . . . I love it still, with all of my heart and mind.

A Closer Look

Linus Lawrence Platt

Editors' note: Linus Lawrence Platt has a background rooted firmly in the climbing world. During the 1980s and '90s and early 2000s, he was active as a climber throughout America and Canada. Looking for a life outside of climbing, in April 2011 he set out from Moab, Utah, by bicycle and headed for Alaska. Dissatisfied that he hadn't experienced enough adventure on his first trip and with an "acute taste for the Yukon," he set out again in May 2013 on another Alaskan bicycle odyssey. In this piece, he describes his two solo journeys. He is a writer, photographer, adventurer, and carpenter. He shares his stories and photographs on his blog Just Rolling By (justrollingby.com). After having lived in Moab for more than twenty years, he now calls Haines, Alaska, his home.

I first fell in love with Alaska when I was 15. Having grown up in California, Alaska seemed as far away and as wild as any place on Earth. I'd heard of this land when I was even younger, perhaps eight or nine, when my father and his brother decided to drive to the Great White North to "check it out." My Dad and Uncle never made it to Alaska, but the notion that it was an endless wilderness full of giant mountains, feral people, and wild animals was born in my young mind. When I was 15, as a young neophyte climber, I read as many books about mountaineering and rock climbing as I could; these books spoke of faraway places and faraway ideas that left deep impressions on me. One such book was Art Davidson's *Minus 148*, a tale of the groundbreaking, first winter ascent of Denali. It was this read that left on me an ironed-in impression of Alaska.

Over the years, as mountaineering became less and less important to me, I began to realize that my desires to be in the wild places that climbing afforded was as important as ever. Being in the mountains was paramount, and climbing was a mere vehicle. Early on in life I developed a love affair with bicycles, and the notion of traveling long distances on one appealed in the same manner that expedition mountaineering appealed to me in earlier years. So in the summer of '93, I set out from Utah and pedaled to San Francisco via Idaho and Oregon. This journey demonstrated all that I desired: to be self sufficient on a long, physical trip; one that allowed an element of adventure while traveling through high country and mountains. It was an eye opener for what might be possible; and somewhere, in the back of my mind, revelatory ideas about wilderness and ways to travel through it began to hatch. On that trip I began to see and feel something greater in the world than just the routine of human life; to understand a deeper connection to all things wild and free and to appreciate the fact that we, as humans, were actually a part of this great wildness—and not separate from it. The winter of 2010–11 was especially harsh, with record snowfall in many northern areas, and unusually low temperatures. In late April 2011, I set out from my home in Moab, Utah, on my bicycle—bound for Alaska.

—⁓ ⁓—

I pedal north, through Utah and into Wyoming, all the while feeling overwhelming joy that such a trip had finally started. I enter a different world as I pedal into Montana. No longer in the high desert of the past 1,000 miles, I cross a threshold into the beginnings of the Earth's great boreal forests, forests that do not stop until high above the Arctic Circle, 3,300 miles to the north.

I travel on, into British Columbia, and climb into the Canadian Rockies. I enter Alberta, the scene of many past climbing adventures, with people from another time and place. It was magnificent to see, after all these years, the Ice Fields, and all of her adjoining peaks and glaciers, this time armed not with ice axe but with bicycle. The wheels turn, and soon I witness the vast boreal plateau of central British Columbia. I see more black bears than I can count. I roll through Smithers B.C. and marvel at this place, surrounded by glaciers and mighty, salmon-filled rivers. Tribal elders and native fisherman tell me stories of long winters and their anticipation of the upcoming moose hunt. At last, on June 9th, I cross the Skeena River and turn onto the mysterious Cassiar Highway. This road is a westerly alternative to the far more popular Alaska Highway in northern B.C., and gifts mountain scenery and remoteness. My first night on the Cassiar, I pull into an open area and spot a dead grizzly—shot, I presume. I am too fatigued from pedaling a full day of rain to search out another camp. I am gripped by my short-lived but intense paranoia of the bears and sleep with one eye open. Over the next eight days, I experience some of the most remote and incredible scenery visible from a road in North America: fantastic glaciated peaks and valleys, raging rivers and serene lakes, bear, moose, eagles, and every animal the travel brochures promise. The natural balance I see before me brings me to tears, and I think hard on where the human race is heading—and why. Rain falls like it will never stop. Spinning through this much rain . . . this many miles . . . this many hours, instigates bizarre things within my mind. I take a hard look at myself and the world around me.

Days later, past Whitehorse, I flow into the Kluane Range, a wall of peaks guarding the mighty Mount St Elias. Out of these mountains flow some of the largest glaciers in the Western Hemisphere. I journey on, around Kluane Lake, the Yukon's largest. Beyond it, the ecosystem changes yet again, and I see the first of many black spruce taiga forests, the hallmark of the True North. On June 27th, 2011, 59 days after leaving Moab, I enter Alaska.

An Alaskan native once told me, in jest, that the Pacific Northwest of the lower 48 was "a desert." On this day, upon penetrating the Alaskan border, a rain begins to fall that is everything that man implied. And for the next five days, that's indeed what it does—with no end in sight. The setting up and taking down of the tent, the moisture consuming my sleeping bag, and the inability to keep or get anything dry, begins to take its toll on me. Worst of all, now nearing the Alaska Range, the storm obscures views of the peaks I came so far to see. I turn south on the Richardson Highway, the clouds part, and for the first time in what seems like eternity, the sun bares brightly and the glaciers of the Central Alaska Range shine deep within me.

I learn, from a woman in Delta Junction, that a narrow two-track leads some 50 miles south, into an area known as Rainbow Ridge, and that an excursion there would reward me with access to the Canwell Glacier and the lesser but enormously beautiful peaks of the Eastern Alaska Range. After some time scouting, I spy the two-track, and head off into the innards of the Alaska I really want to see. I ride and push the bike back far from the highway, perhaps eight or nine miles, until I come to the lateral moraine of the glacier. I camp perched atop the moraine, overlooking the ice. I am home. The next day, as fine as the one prior, I embark on a scramble up a nearby granite peak, surrounded by nameless glaciers and tundra. The sensation of this magical place sinks into me, and there is no turning back.

A day later I join the Denali Highway, 135 miles of dirt road traversing some of the finest wilderness in North America. I slow down, breath deeply, and take it all in. I spend four days out there marveling at the grand peaks of Mounts Hayes, Hess, and Deborah, eventually turning south on the Park's Highway and heading toward Talkeetna and Anchorage. As I move south, I feel civilization creeping in on me. I know that the part of this journey to encompass supreme wilderness is nearing closure.

I had pedaled more than 3,800 miles, and on August 9th, I board the Marine Vessel *Columbia* for a trip down the whimsical Inside Passage, ending port at Bellingham, Washington. I spend the next two weeks pedaling down the coasts of Washington, Oregon, and California. This is another world to me—cities, towns, cars, traffic lights, and difficult camp spots, at least in comparison to Alaska, where I could easily push my bike into any section of woods and have my own palace for the evening. Within the cities of central California, I feel trapped and overwhelmed. I long for the quiet and solitude that Alaska affords. After 4,700 miles, this trip is over with a quickness. What I really want is to get back to Alaska and spend less time getting there, and more time being there. I crave a closer look.

Settling down in Sacramento for the winter to visit family and earn money for my return to Alaska was in order. The unfortunate event of having my bicycle stolen the following spring, just one month prior to my planned departure date, thwarted all that I had worked toward and my dreams of returning that summer were shattered. I kept my head up and pushed on, hanging tough through the next 12 months and creating a tight and sound itinerary for the following summer; I developed an acute taste for the Yukon during this time, and wanted to see more of it.

It's May 2013. I drive my pickup to Bellingham, park at a friend's house, and board another marine vessel, this time heading north to Skagway, Alaska.

The first day I face the biggest climb of the entire trip: from sea level at Skagway to the summit of 2,864-foot White Pass at the B.C. border. I offload the ship, and dive into the dragon's mouth. By dusk, I make the pass and have my tent set up in time to enjoy the alpenglow cover the glaciers to the east. It is May 20th, 2013, and it feels surreal to be back, as if I never left, but merely awakened from a long dreamy nap. I pedal up the Klondike Highway, passing through Whitehorse and embarking on many side trips down old mining roads in search of beautiful campsites, old cabins, wild rivers, grizzly bears, and eagles. I find all of these things in the Yukon and much, much more. About two days south of Dawson City, I spot a large mammal ahead on the shoulder. I slow down and approach cautiously. At first, I take it to be a small black bear, but it doesn't move like a bear. It dances and darts in a way that tells me only one thing: wolf. As I move closer, it sees me and flies into the brush. As I move past, I can still see its legs behind the shrubbery, moving laterally with me. I stop. The wolf stops. I move and the wolf darts back out, into sight. We stop. We lock eyes. I am mesmerized by this magnificent animal. It appears to be an older wolf, perhaps lone, his coat thick from a recent cold winter, his color nearly solid black. We tire of this staring contest and in a flash, the wolf is gone. The next day, I spot a large grizzly on a nearby ridge, digging for food. It is far away, but its motion and heft clearly demonstrate its kind.

In 2011, I had developed a hunger to visit the Arctic. To me, the Arctic represents the last bastion of real wilderness on the planet. It is a place that few travel, and it is a place that, for all of its supreme ruggedness, remains one of the most fragile places on earth. I imagined it to be one of the most beautiful as well. I had to get there.

I roll into Dawson City, centerpiece for the historical mining heralds of the Yukon, past and present. It is May 28th, which means that it is still very early in the season for travel into remote regions where the Dempster Highway leads, but not impossible. If I am to embark on a trip up the 500 miles of dirt road on the Dempster, there might be weather and road conditions that are not favorable. But to me, it seems perfect.

After spending a day in Dawson, I decide the only way to do this stretch is to do it round-trip—1,000 miles total. The Dempster ends at the village of Inuvik, Northwest Territories, where one can buy food and supplies, but the two villages on the way are situated along the road as to make carrying the necessary food impractical. To alleviate this matter, I box up four days' worth of food and leave it at the Dempster Interpretive Center in the hope that a traveler might pick it up and take it to Eagle Plains, some 300 miles to the north. I spend the day gathering the remainder of supplies for a venture into a fantastic arena of mountains and Arctic plains. In the morning, I pedal the 25 miles to the start of the Dempster and am pinned down by a several-hour rainstorm that began calmly enough, but was soon a torrential downpour of monstrous proportions. I hole up at a defunct gas station at the junction of said road, and eat and drink to pass the time. Over the next two days, I cross the Tombstone Mountains and enter the Blackstone uplands, famous for its crossing of the mighty Porcupine caribou herd, which, during its migration through the region, numbers in the high thousands. Passing the Continental Divide, the terrain is of an alpine nature for which I am most happy. From here, all water from these mountains flow to the Mackenzie River, and ultimately, the Arctic Ocean. More rain comes and I dive into the Engineer Creek Campground, which is still closed for the season. The place is deserted. It has a screened in cook hut and a luxurious evening was to be had. The following morning, I cross the Ogilvie River, and see an unfortunate sign ahead: "Road Closed." I sneak past the closure in hopes of somehow working myself and my bicycle around whatever obstacle lies ahead, but a road worker chases me down.

"Can't you read?" he asks.

"Yes, Sir. I can read just fine," I say.

As I attempt to keep pedaling, he whips his truck in front of me and informs me that *no one* will pass.

"The river has changed course from flooding and has taken out the road," he says. "Go back to Engineer Creek and hole up there 'til I send word you can continue."

Reluctantly, I turn around, head back to the campground, and down the last couple of beers I had stashed. In the morning, a truck pulls in and some folks from Washington inform me they have heard that it will be several days before the situation is rectified. I feel sunk. I don't have enough food to stay here sitting and waiting. They offer me a ride the 130 miles back to Dawson and I sheepishly accept. That night in Dawson, I wrestle with the situation. Had I made the right decision? Could I have stretched the food I had? I put it all behind me and go to bed, hoping I won't be discovered illegally camped on the outskirts of town. After breaking camp, I board the ferry across the omnipotent Yukon River, and commit myself to what's known as the "Top of the World" highway: a hundred or so miles of gravel traversing the hilly, sub-Arctic dome country of the western Yukon and eastern Alaska. The monotony of the endless forest and the ever-growing number of hills are hurting me, but I manage to get across the Alaska border the next day.

More rain ensues. More spectacular scenery begins to appear. Great, wild rivers paralleling this stretch of the Taylor Highway begin to cheer me up, and soon the Dempster/Top of the World episode is behind me. Near the junction of the Taylor and Alaska Highways, about 30 miles from Tok, I crest a hill, and as if on cue, the clouds part, and the sun shines down upon the ever-magnificent Alaska Range. I feel, once again, as if I'd come home. The mountains appear almost Himalayan in size and give me the sensation of seeing an old friend. I spend a couple of nights in Tok, then pedal along the northern and eastern flats below the looming Alaska Range. The creeks are plentiful and crystal clear, and I drink copious amounts of water. It's another night of thunderstorms, and I pack up in a morning rain. It is getting to be routine.

I find myself able to pack it in with my eyes closed. Later in the day when the sun is out, I pull out the tent fly and it dries while I snack.

In Delta Junction, I camp on the gravel beaches of the wildly braided Tanana River, looking to the south at the appearance the central Alaska Range's Mounts Deborah, Hayes, and Hess. All are visible. I have never seen the north side of these peaks. I decide to camp here in hopes of catching a time-lapse of these giants in the morning, with the sunlight splattered across their eastern escarpment and embellishing their glacial armor. The scene before me stirs my desires for reaching the Arctic again.

There are only two roads, in North America, that one might pilot a vehicle of some sort, leading to this continent's Arctic areas. The Yukon's Dempster Highway and the Dalton Highway, aka "The Haul Road," in Alaska. Both of these paths are of the dirt and gravel variety. The Haul Road, remote indeed, was built in 1974 as a supply line to the North Slope oil fields at the Arctic Ocean, and parallels the Trans-Alaska Pipeline, and was not open to use by the general public until 1996. Up to that point, the truckers had it to themselves. The Haul Road traverses a rugged landscape north of Fairbanks and leads to Deadhorse, Alaska, crossing terrain varying from the forested hill and dome country beginning at Fairbanks to taiga swamps and open tundra, crosses many, many rivers and streams, and penetrates the "Alaskan Rockies"—the Continental Divide at the bastion of true roadless Alaskan wilderness: the venerable Brooks Range.

Saturday morning I gear up, and soon my bicycle is spinning north. The day is filled with some of the worst hill climbing I have ever encountered. Finally crossing Snowshoe Summit at the apex of Alaska's White Mountains, I am rewarded with a long downhill and a stream of spring water shooting from a pipe near the road's edge. The water is clear, cold, and delicious. Passing creeks and abandoned cabins, I look for a camp, and pull onto a dirt track next to the Tatalina River and, after setting up camp, dive into the water. I am then greeted by terrible swarms of Alaska's famous insect.

The next day, more of the same hill climbing continues, only worse this time. The hills are 12 to 14 percent, made up of loose, unconsolidated gravel, and the truck traffic is thick. This day turned out to be the hardest of the entire road. By day's end, I am so exhausted, I can do nothing but dismount the bike and push the dead beast upward and over the hilltops, coast down the other side and repeat. More big hills the following morning lead, thankfully, to the Yukon River, where once across, the road flattens out a bit and some pristine forested Alaskan countryside sprouts up. Eventually, however, the hills reappear and the grind continues. After 70 miles, I find a gravel pit to call home on the fringe of Finger Mountain, 25 miles south of the Arctic Circle. The first bits of Arctic tundra, permafrost meltwater lakes, tors of granite, and windswept mountain passes are now within my eyesight. The next day, the landscape changes dramatically. It's the type of high country I so desire. After crossing the Arctic Circle, I penetrate a small mountain pass and catch my first glimpse of the mighty Brooks Range. I drop into the valley below, and am greeted with magnificent spruce forest and creeks filled with 24-inch Grayling. There is drinking water everywhere, a far cry from the relative dryness of the last few days out of Fairbanks. This landscape is what I came here for . . . unparalleled high country filled with rivers, mountains, forest, and animals.

In the morning, I'm excited to get into the Brooks Range. After a couple of hours pedaling through soaring scenery, I decide to get off Haul Road proper and onto the pipeline access road, which offers a bit more of the deep solitude that this unbelievable place offers. Eventually the road dead-ends as the pipeline disappears underground, which dictates backtracking to the Haul Road a couple of miles. However, at its end, a spectacular campsite is to be had, on the Koyakuk, and facing a sunset view of the mighty southwest face of Sukakpak Mountain, an impressive chunk of limestone real estate. After swimming in the Koyakuk, I set up the camera for an evening time-lapse of Sukakpak's dramatic episode of color and changing light.

A fine morning follows, and along with it 40 miles of dead flat, yet gorgeous scenery. The river is heavily braided; the forest begins to thin out. Signs of a changing ecosystem, of a different stature, unfold. The weather begins to change, too. Thunderclouds build, then unleash; I retreat under a bridge and watch the storm from beneath, sitting next to river ice pack still 36 inches thick today, June 20th. A few short miles and I pass the final spruce tree in this part of North America. It is all tundra and the road begins to climb. Up I go. The road flattens once again onto the spectacular Chandalar Shelf, a couple of hundred square miles of flat tundra in the heart of the Brooks, just below the Continental Divide at Atigun Pass, Alaska's highest and most northerly road pass at 4,800 feet. As I near Atigun's summit, the storm once again decides to unleash its fury. High winds, sideways rain, and plummeting temperatures commence. I top out at 9:30 pm and find a patch of snow-free tundra a ways off the road and pitch my tent—right there on Atigun's high point. Even with the tent heavily guyed, I still have to brace it from the inside to prevent the poles from snapping. Finally, the wind dies off and I drift to sleep, dreaming that night of being deeper in this range of magic mountains in the North, father in than I am now, traveling high valleys among grizzly bear and caribou.

I awake to a deeply silent atmosphere of near-whiteout conditions; it is eerily calm. I pack up, and descend the pass slightly to the shelf on the north side and stop for a hike up to a ridge. The tundra here is squat and is easily traveled. It is crowded with tiny wildflowers of all shapes and colors. I pass the remains of a young caribou, probably taken by wolves. Farther up, I glimpse down great gullies of rock towards a massive creek with outstanding waterfalls feeding its descent into the Atigun River and beyond to the Arctic Ocean. The peaks are mere 6,000 footers, but they are massive just the same. The Brooks is a dry region. There are a few small glaciers scattered in a couple of places in the Brooks, but not here. There are thin gullies of snow descending from the rocky summits of these peaks, providing a striking contrast to their nearly black and orange coloring. Eventually, I descend back to the bike, and continue on, down Atigun Canyon, and onto the great Arctic Plains of Alaska's North Slope.

The next two days are flat tussock tundra, starkly beautiful, and swelling with my favorite insects. I still see no bears, but, plenty of fox and caribou. Alas, I spot a herd of musk ox, 20 strong, prehistoric, ice-age creatures of the North American Arctic, an iconic figure of strength and endurance in this vast, untamed Arctic landscape.

The next day, rolling into Deadhorse, it is 28 degrees with 40-mile-per-hour winds, but otherwise uneventful. Deadhorse is the center of North America's largest oilfield, which stretches for more than 70 miles to the west. After a fitful night's sleep, I pedal out of town a couple of miles, lay the bike down, and put out my thumb . . . Later, after no success in hitching a ride, I catch an hour and a half flight to Fairbanks, where in a couple of weeks, my lover, friend, and companion, Angela, is to meet up with me and we will continue the last legs of this journey, together.

These long bicycle trips had, until this point, always been done solo. Angela coming aboard for this adventure is new territory for me. It will be a new and wonderful experience to share this monumental place with her. A tough and beautiful soul, she also shares a desire for all things wild and free, and is a lover of animals, mountains, and lakes. She has never been to Alaska, and I will be proud to show her what I know of this endless, magical place. On the late night of August 2, Angela, driving my truck up from Bellingham, pulls into Fairbanks, and within 24 hours, we are ready to go. Angela, now riding the bike that I rode on that first trip back in '93, is out to prove that old bikes don't really die. I painted it green some time back, just before giving it to her. She set forth calling the machine "The Green Bastard" after Bubbles's superhero character in the Canadian film *Trailer Park Boys*.

We leave Fairbanks at three in the afternoon on August 4, and still manage to pedal 34 miles to a nice woods camp in the Nenana Hills. The forest is a splendid place to be as the past two weeks of being in Fairbanks had been wearing thin upon me. After a hearty supper and a victory cocktail, we fall into a deep sleep that only two tired yet happy people can achieve. Pedaling the next few days brings us to Nenana, Healy, and McKinley Park. On the third of those days, a car, speeding up behind me, veers onto the shoulder and nearly kills me. That night at a peaceful lakeside camp just north of Cantwell, we watch as the sun sets behind the western rim and an alpenglow on the opposing peaks highlights a small herd of Dall sheep, clinging wildly to the upper slopes. After entering the Alaska Range, we sail into Cantwell, beginning of the glorious Denali Highway, and the opening for some of the most fantastic scenery Alaska has to offer.

The Denali Highway, which I had pedaled two years before, was built in 1957. For many years prior to the highway's completion, it was the only way to approach Denali National Park, hence its name. The road is 135 miles long and connects Cantwell to Paxson. One hundred and twenty miles of that are dirt and gravel. The DH, as I call it, traverses the entire Central Alaska Range, crosses uncountable streams and rivers, and features tundra, forest, mountains, and lakes aplenty. It also has some of the best free-range camping anywhere. It is a true mountain paradise. We roll out onto the welcome relief of the gravel and with the exception of the dust from occasional traffic, we sail smoothly along the grandiose Alaska Range, surrounded by tundra, taiga, and wilderness. We spy a two track leading into the forest and think there might be a reward at its end. We ride through beautiful forest and brush, spotting a large bull caribou along the way.

After a mile or so, the forest thins and the road turns downward to gain the roaring river below. Here, at this transition, lies one of the most spectacular camp spots of our lives. It is an open view of all the big peaks of the range: Mounts Hess, Hayes, Deborah, Geist, Balchen, and Shand.

Having recently read David Robert's *Deborah: A Wilderness Narrative*, I was especially happy to be enjoying this spectacular place again. In front of us are towering peaks encompassing one of the great wilderness regions on the continent. Watching the sun set upon this picture, with its hues of red and orange mixed with the deep blue of the glaciers in front of us, is something we will not soon forget.

The following morning it is raining. We commit to the mud, and soon the McClaren River Lodge comes around and we drop in for a beer and a snack. We leave the lodge during a brief interlude in the storm, and climb the thousand feet to the summit. We are exhausted and wet, and it's raining solidly. We ride down the two track of the McClaren Summit trail, and throw our nylon ghetto down onto the soft and sopping tundra and dive into the tent. In the morning, it is still raining, but our spirits are high as we prepare for the last day on the DH. Cool temperatures and more rain bring us to the pavement 20 miles from Paxson, signaling the end of the highway. We stop at the Paxson Lodge for a spell and some dry time. The weather finally clears for our pedal down the Richardson in search of another fine Alaskan camp.

We awake the next morning to outstanding weather and an early start sends us down the Richardson Highway to the Gulkana River for an afternoon of bathing and river laundry. It feels good to be in the river, the sun overhead and our clothing, now clean, drying on the clothesline I've rigged. Unfortunately, the camp is very moist, and our clothing doesn't dry till noon the following day, which puts us on the road late. It works out for the best, as we roll into a fine camp early in the day. It is extraordinary, consisting of perfect, flat forest right next to a steep 300-foot embankment that drops to the mighty Copper River below, infested with salmon and running ever so strong. It also sports unobstructed views of Mounts Sanford, Drum, Wrangell, and the enormous Mount Blackburn—all encased in glacial ice, and all piercing the deep blue, cloudless sky. To me, it is a camp to behold. The Wrangell Mountains are a special place to me. They are remote, and, according to some bush pilots I spoke with, the most beautiful place in all Alaska

We continue onward, down the Richardson, and turn in on the old Elliott cutoff, a dirt track leading for 10 miles, to the hamlet of Kenny Lake, an area of rare Alaskan agriculture featuring, pigs, yaks, chickens, and pastures. We stock up on a thing or two at the tiny store, and continue en route to Chitina. We roll on through, eager to get ourselves established on the dirt and gravel of the McCarthy Road, and away from the troublesome traffic. Crossing the Copper River Bridge, we are greeted with a fine, Alaskan sight: the confluence of the Copper and Chitina Rivers, the Chugach Mountains to the south, the Wrangells to the north, and the dipnetters, still pulling late season Reds from the icy waters. I catch fine glimpses of the enormous Mount Blackburn, at 16,390 feet the sixth highest peak in Alaska.

The McCarthy Road is blessed with many small creeks and rivers, all crystal-clear specimens, born of the ice and flowing to the sea. There are fewer lakes, however. Angela feels at peace when she is swimming in a lake, so we are always keeping our eyes peeled for an opportunity to do so. Farther up Long Lake appears, and Angela declares the place her spiritual home. Unfortunately, we find no spot to camp on its shores, but a nearby site is available, with the best loon calls I've ever heard. Salmon enter the lake to spawn, attracting bears that snag their lunch. The next day is a fine one; with perfect weather it is a short pedal to McCarthy and we were rolling through town by noon. About a half mile before reaching the tiny village, we are greeted by a splendid sight. In front of us lie the Kennicott and Root Glaciers, both giants and flowing from towering peaks. As the rivers of ice rise to their birth places above the firn line, an enormous icefall, the "Staircase Icefall" as it is known, shows itself. It's a sea of jumbled and towering ice blocks and seracs, all destined to crumble and become a part of the glacier below.

We find McCarthy more than pleasing: a tiny town full of laid-back folks, tourists, flight seers, bush pilots, and mountain folk. We buy a few groceries at the unexpected store, and chat with a few folks before departing to find a camp. A local tells us of a trail that leads to the toe of the Kennicott Glacier, and we head out. After getting temporarily lost, we find our way and are rewarded by a great field of gravel, ice, and water. The Kennicott's tarn, the size of an Alaskan air strip, is under constant barrage from its gravel-covered ice source just above, and great splashes can be heard every so often. We camp near the shores of the tarn and admire the unbelievable glacial view from our camp. Later, we hike out, away from the tent, to inspect bear prints Angela had spotted earlier.

A day of hiking is in order and we pedal up the road, past the Kennicott Copper Mine, once the largest copper operation in North America. Passing through the mine area, we continue on a deteriorating trail, park the bikes, and continue on foot. Following the Root Glacier, we hike five or six miles up the valley and find a place that looks reasonable to descend. Down we go, crawling across scree-covered ice hills to reach the main body of ice. Angela has never been on a glacier, and it had been a while since I had been on one of this size. We step out onto the flat ice, well below the firn line, and small, but open crevasses appear. A giant moulin is flowing wildly upon the giant's back and we drink freely from its source. We climb back up the loose scree to the trail and skedaddle downvalley to our bikes. A quick blast back to McCarthy takes only minutes and soon we are in camp again. That night, very late, I get up and a slight tinge of the Aurora Borealis appears. Summer is coming to an end.

The following day is Angela's birthday, and it is raining badly. We take cover in the local coffee shack and put off getting into the mud till past noon. The day is spent mostly in wet conditions and endless, grinding mud. This signals the end of my bottom bracket, rear hub, and drivetrain. My bicycle is very tired indeed. The next few days are spent pedaling south on the Richardson Highway, crossing the fantastic Thompson Pass en route to Valdez where we catch the ferry to Whittier and pedal to Anchorage. Angela and I say our goodbyes, which is hard since I will not see her again for five months, as I am staying the winter in Alaska. She boards a plane bound for the "outside," as Alaskans are sometimes fond of calling the lower 48, and I, catching a rare and outstanding view of Denali from the Glenn Highway, shift back into gear, and pedal north, in search of another fine Alaskan camp.

Across America on a Harley-Davidson

Robyn Davidson

*Editors' note: Robyn Davidson is one of the greatest adventurers Aus-
tralia has produced. She grew up on a cattle station in southeastern
Queensland. In the late 1970s she moved to Alice Springs for two years
to work with camels for a trek she was planning—from Alice to the
Indian Ocean, across some of the harshest terrain on earth. The subsequent nine-month journey via 1,700 miles of Australian outback captured the attention of the world and became a cover story for* National
Geographic. *The worldwide interest in her adventure (she had never
intended to write about her journey) prompted her to write* Tracks *(in
Doris Lessing's London home), which became an international bestseller. She later became a cultural anthropologist and studied nomadic
cultures in India and Tibet. In 2013 a film about her outback adventure directed by John Curran and starring Mia Wasikowska was made.
Her other books include* Tracks, Australia: Beyond the Dreamtime,
Ancestors, Desert Places, *and* The Picador Book of Journeys. *This
story, about traveling across the United States on a Harley-Davidson,
is excerpted from her 1993 book* Travelling Light.

There is no stretch of highway in the world more boring than
Route 75 through Ohio. After hours of staring at soggy flat farm-
land, from the back of a Harley-Davidson, through billowing
truck fumes and drizzle, my first glimpse of the truck stop cafe
was a welcome, if surreal, relief. The American mid-west breakfast
of two eggs, bacon, sausages, hominy grits, french fries, pancakes,

carcinogens and sodium nitrite was to keep us alive until we reached California, where, miraculously, as soon as you crossed the border, you began eating beansprouts, whole-wheat bread and spinach salad with blue cheese dressing.

There were at least 200 trucks parked outside this three-acre extravaganza. Truck drivers who wore ten-gallon hats, T-shirts ("I'd rather push my Harley than ride a rice-burner"), turquoise and silver belt buckles, and snakeskin boots with toes so pointed they could open envelopes, jostled for position at the food counter, or crowded into the space-invader rooms, or riffled through back-copies of *Easyriders* in the reading rooms, or quaffed beer in the bars, or filled their tanks at the forest of gas pumps. Everything a truckie ever wanted or needed was there, including cowboy-booted squaw-tasselled truck-groupies hanging provocatively and vacantly around the doors. Our breakfast neighbour eyed us suspiciously until he found out we were from Australia. "What's it like livin' in one of them goddamn socialist countries? I hear tell you can't even carry guns there. Man, I couldn't live without mah guns."

Since leaving New York, three weeks before, we'd been living out a "Leave it to Beaver" re-run. I don't think I could have tackled it without my genuine, padded, press-studded, black leather Harley-Davidson motorcycle jacket. Not only did I walk taller when I had it on, and feel meaner and look tougher, but the human sea in the streets of Manhattan parted before me. It was, as a leftie journalist had said when the first space shuttle went up, "biblical, man."

And after the torment of a three-week publicity tour, I needed any props I could get. When I wasn't collapsing in Hyatt hotel rooms, or being powdered up for chat shows, or fearing for my life on aeroplanes, I was holed up in the cavernous splendour of a white, well-appointed loft in Soho, where chemically fed pot-plants watched my back; where subdued jazz played on the FM;

where endless replays of Reagan getting shot (his theatrical piece de resistance), interspersed with doctors' reports and static, played on the TV; where sirens played on the streets; where there were two phones with buttons and dials and red flashing lights, neither of which I knew how to work; where the taps required an IQ of 500 to be turned on; where rows of fumbly security locks on the front door, lift buttons, lift door and apartment door did nothing for my paranoia because any thug could climb up the fire escape and break a window; and where there were only frozen orange juice, Best Foods mayonnaise and fifty rolls of film in the fridge, because everyone ate out. Except me.

So I rang Steve, who joined me from London a week later. When he suggested we buy a motorcycle and ride from New York to California, where he was born and raised, but hadn't seen for ten years, I barely put up a struggle. The thought of wind in my hair, the freedom of the open road, and dying instantly under the wheels of a Mack truck seemed almost appealing. The only things I had against the idea were the possibilities of either spending the rest of my life feeding mashed bananas to a quadriplegic or waking up in some mid-west hospital, unable to remember my own name. There was also in me a deep resistance to being second in command. If Isabelle Eberhardt—that eccentric Victorian wanderer—hit the nail on the head with "life on the open road is the essence of freedom," she qualified that with "no one is free who is not alone." Quite.

And I was ignorant of bikes. I didn't like them. I had no intention of ever learning to ride one. I didn't even understand bikie language. Riding to me has always meant a relationship with an animal—horse, donkey, camel even. You don't ride a machine, you sit on it. Nor was I good "bikie moll" material. Good bikie molls sit on the back and keep their traps shut. They don't whinge. They aren't back-seat drivers. When the bike breaks down, they don't blame the driver, er, rider. There was a lot I had to learn.

It was raining when we went to pick up the gleaming black and silver sin machine. It sat at the back of the shop like a poisonous insect. While Steve talked with the proprietors about teflon sprockets and eighty-cubic-inch shovelheads, I strolled around the accessories. Was this an S and M outfitters or what? I picked out the most expensive helmet (I like my brains where they are) and then my gaze alighted on the leather jackets. I took one out, tried it on and, hey presto, transmogrification. I placed my fag between my lips, squinted through the smoke, put my thumbs in my pockets and ambled back to the guys. They spoke to me! I now understood how the invisible man felt when he put his bandages on. "Great deeds and great thoughts," as Camus said, "all have a ridiculous beginning."

Ah, the intoxication of speed as we hurtled from beneath the broken teeth of Manhattan's skyline and onto the freeway. After the first thirty miles, I started loosening up. Enjoying it even. There was, after all, some pleasure in not being the one in control. My limpet-like clutchings, the involuntary shutting of the eyes when we leaned into a corner, were being replaced by stunts: the standing up on the pegs to give fist salutes to other bikers, the leaning back on the sissy bar to roll a smoke, and the moving from cheek to cheek to relieve the growing numbness in my bottom. After a hundred miles the discomfort was intense, the grumbling loud. Harley-Davidsons are not designed for the comfort of the bit-of-rag on the back, they are designed for the comfort of the rider, and for style. I was hunched on a stylish vibrating fence-post and feeling resentful.

I tapped Stevie on the shoulder (he was singing "I just wanna ride on my motorcyyyyy-cle." Could this regressed maniac be the man who had seen me through thick and thin in London?) and asked him to stop at the next sports shop. We were bound for Vermont, and there were no sports shops. There were drug stores, which sold invalid's inflatable toilet seats. I had no shame; I bought one. I was willing to risk my credibility with the bike fraternity, but my buttocks, never. I grew very attached to that cushion over the next three months. If Flann O'Brien was right about molecular transference, then Steve was becoming more like a bike, and I was turning into . . .

We rode ten hours that day, across the Adirondacks, around the swooping bends of Lake Champlain, through the first sweet hints of spring—polluted only by those totems to the American Dream: the omnipresent cars and billboards, the gas stations, the baseball caps and the fast-food franchises. America is a car culture, constantly travelling to greener pastures. Americans do not see the horror, junk and pain littering the way. There is always a new frontier to head for, so how much you bugger up the one you're on is irrelevant. This faith in the future at the expense of the present comes from moving fast with the windows wound up.

By the time we arrived at our friends' country house just outside Hinesburg, we were exhausted. We couldn't talk. We drooled. They put us to bed. I was too tired to attack Steve for bringing me on this torturous and pointless journey. But after three days with them, during which we gum-booted our way through Vermont's mud season (apparently not its finest) and stuffed ourselves with home-made apple pies, and swapped vitriolic reminiscences of book tours and reviewers, the desire to be off hunting for new frontiers began to infect me too. The first burst of acceleration as you leave somewhere in the early morning is almost worth the increasing tedium of the following miles.

Our plan was to head for Canada, turn south, then follow the setting sun. But when the first flakes of jet-stream snow bit into my face, I knew it was a rotten idea. We put all our clothes on, till we looked like marshmallows, and wrapped scarves around our faces, but still we could travel no more than twenty miles without having to stop for coffee to thaw out. We decided to go due west to Ohio.

Now, all this time I had been pestering Steve about camping out. Motels were expensive and, anyway, I wanted to sleep next to the earth and watch the constellations and build warming fires and sing songs and communicate a little with Mother Nature, whom I hadn't seen in quite a while. "I think you'll find camping out in this country a little disappointing after what you've been used to," was all Steve had said. I couldn't imagine what he'd meant. Camping out is camping out. It's driving off the road into the bush and looking for wood and boiling tea and giving in to pantheism. How could that be different anywhere?

After gasping and gagging through Detroit air, I insisted that we stop at a camping spot the map showed us on the shores of one of the Great Lakes, thirty miles outside that blighted city. It was getting dark, but still Mother Nature was nowhere in sight. Just more black slums and a nuclear power plant. Yes, our camping spot was a patch of mown grass, nestled beneath this glittering structure, and just off the freeway. There was no wood. There were no trees. Just rows of trucks and vans parked on the grass. The entrance fee was eight dollars. This barren patch of horror was second home to whites who could no longer find work in the city and were now employed by the plant. They saw their families on weekends. They were worried.

We rolled out our sleeping bag a little way from the edge of the lake. Decaying rubber thongs, used condoms and dead fish littered its putrescent shores. Vile garbage smells wafted into our puckered nostrils; repetitive clangings of nuclear reactor machinery sang us to sleep. We had entered the throbbing heart of the American nightmare.

By the time we reached Kentucky, the graffiti in the ladies' toilets had changed. No longer the simple sexual references, or the diagrammatic genitalia. Even the "I love Bud" scribblings and the arrowed hearts gave way to purely religious references and fire and brimstone sentiments as the southern accents grew thicker.

However, the blue grass country was indeed beautiful, the weather was warm, and my spirits were thawing. We stopped in at a diner for a BLT sandwich and a beer.

That tiny backwoods diner was the antithesis of the dreaded Ohio truck stop. It had the best jukebox I've ever come across: Howlin' Wolf, Bo Diddley, Mance Lipscomb, and some of the most obscure and brilliant country and western I've heard. When we told the waitress that we were taking the Harley to California, and thence to Australia, she looked wistful, then puzzled and uncertain. "Well, ain't that somethin'. I always had the ah-dea there was some water twixt us and them." By the time we reached Tennessee the graffiti was not only biblical but racist as well.

Everyone has been told horror stories about the south. Steve said that during the sixties he'd been run out of towns he'd had no intention of stopping in. But we not only had no trouble, we were treated with utmost courtesy. Even the Harley, an erstwhile symbol of the evils of northern degeneracy, got some appreciative comments.

Things had certainly changed. The south suffered such a whipping during the civil rights movement, so much bad press had taken the heat off the north, which was equally guilty of repression, and which was still ripping it off economically, that the southerners were now bending over backwards to prove, especially to foreigners, that they were just regular friendly folks. And if that friendliness never got beyond the "have a nice day" level, if that friendliness was only a millimetre thick, beneath which lay the stuff fanatics and Queenslanders are made of, we were never around long enough to worry about it. We spoke to very few blacks. They cast their eyes downwards, smiled apologetically and crossed the street before any contact could be made. Not here the cocky confidence of New York blacks.

One night, on the banks of the gurgling Mississippi, our appreciation of the southern mystique deepened. The campground was a gravel pit and, because the freeway was only a few yards away, we had difficulty sleeping. Eventually we unplugged our ears and listened to our neighbours—a plucky little Nashville crooner and his sad, monosyllabic wife. Spotlighted by the bulb that dangled outside the cement toilet block, they were singing Hank Williams born-again songs to the tinny accompaniment of a plug-in guitar, and passing the baseball cap around to the lumber-jack-shirted occupants of three Ford pick-ups, all of which had bibles and rifles in the back.

We learnt when to interject with "praise the Lords" and "hal-lelujahs" while a pretty fourteen-year-old girl, all painted up for her big night out, sat among the rifles, bibles and men, and did not move, speak or breathe as they cracked smutty sexual and nigger jokes and slurped Cokes and sang gospel songs. Even such inroads to an understanding of what lurks beneath southern hospitality could not tempt me into dallying. Truth and Consequence, New Mexico, was still a long way off, and anything might happen.

Something did: my first Oklahoma tornado.

I'd been sitting on my cushion, watching rainclouds gather, wondering if I was going to get wet as well as bored, and mull-ing over the difficulty of coming to grips with the meaning of life on the back of a bullet travelling through ever-changing visual stimulae.

It's not that there isn't ample time to think—it's that it's usu-ally on the level of what you are going to eat for lunch. Persig or no Persig, here was no inward journey. When you ride a machine, you are always on your way to somewhere, you are never actually "there." When you walk, you are always "there" and can never get away from "there." It gives you time to ponder and be changed.

On a machine you are protected from change. That, after all, is potentially revolutionary, and there is little room left for that in America, where whole communities set off in roving bands of mobile homes with appropriate names like "The Invader," taking not only their colour televisions and kitchen sinks with them, but also their neighbours. For all America's reverence of individualism, it is of the strictly manipulable kind.

I was jolted from this reverie by a claw-like black cloud scudding across the plains. My, but that cloud is travelling fast, I thought. Suddenly there were swarms of clouds, boiling clouds, furious clouds. We were on a freeway—the next exit was a few miles on. Stevie revved the bike until we were zooming through the most electrifying spectacle I had ever witnessed. Until, that is, I spied the funnel.

For all those who have not turned off an American freeway on to a dirt road at 120 miles per hour, don't try it. Unless, of course, you are being chased by a black, lightning-fringed finger of death. We escaped it—just—and spent the next few hours in a tiny village called Pink, sheltering from the hail and violent winds. Nothing like a bit of adrenalin to bring you back to reality. We stayed a couple of days with an oil-drilling friend in Norman, but I was anxious to get to the deserts, where I was sure a gnawing sense of displacement would be cured.

There are many good reasons for visiting the States, but, to my mind, the two that stand out like Manhattan's twin towers are tasting, for the first time in your life—in a down-at-heel roadside restaurant on the outskirts of a ghost town whose name you will never remember—real Mexican food and real Margaritas, and seeing, also for the first time in your life, the astonishing wonderland of the south-western deserts. Put them together, add a bike and good weather, a soupçon of snow-capped mountains in the distance, and you've a recipe for hedonistic joy.

Perhaps it was the sudden injection of chilli rellenos, tequila and vitamins, perhaps it was the high altitude, piney-woods country of Arizona, perhaps it was the sniff of the arid zone that made my spirits soar but, whatever it was, by the time we flew through those vistas of limitless forest, rolling green into grey into blue, I was feeling on top of the world. By now I had replaced my helmet with a scarf—had become a convert, in fact, to the anti-helmet-law lobby (because, let's face it, if you do bounce off your bike at eighty miles per hour, no feat of engineering ever designed is going to keep your grey matter from spilling). You feel better with it off, you see more, you don't suffer from neck strain, you can hear birdcalls distorted by Doppler effect, and if you're going to be mad enough to ride a bike in the first place, you may as well go the whole hog.

Enough has been written about the marvels of the Grand Canyon, and all of it under-statement. The place is magnificent. But the tourists and the prices began to grate, so we headed for Monument Valley—John Ford country; home of what's left of the Navajo. It was, if anything, even more awesome than the canyon, and to which no film or photograph could do justice. Mile after mile the endless flatness stretched on, interrupted only by towering monoliths of bare rock and the occasional eagle wheeling through the wall of silvery heat shimmer, rising up into blue-black sky. This was what I'd been looking for. This was where the heart was.

While Australian deserts have a more unearthly, prehistoric, mythological quality, while they demand more depth of feeling, the American deserts take the cake for sheer brazen grandiosity and impact. They don't grow on you, they hit you in the back of the head like a mallet. Away from the reservation itself, where we were required to stay on the roads, I was able, for the first time, to sleep in the sand dunes, and to walk out into the desert as far as I could and not see a fence, or a path, or a soul.

Coming from Australia, I had considered this privilege a right. But in America nature was fenced in—under glass. For most people the pleasure of being alone in the wilderness was a thing of the past. The bush had become an alien, dangerous and distant thing. Control is the name of the game, and I wonder how Australia will deal with the same problem, which it eventually must, as all the wild places are taken over by multinationals and tourism. Our extraordinary freedom to move where we like will become the privilege of a select few. This recurring theme, of seeing Australia's future in America's present, was what disturbed me most. That Australia is learning nothing from American mistakes, that we are swallowing all the worst aspects of the dross and spillage of the American Dream.

We strolled along the well-graded National Park paths, and read plaques informing us in large print that some European explorer had discovered the place, and then in small print at the bottom that an unnamed Indian guide had taken him there.

Some things are the same the world over.

Two days later we were surrounded by the chintz and tinsel of Las Vegas. (If you can possibly wean yourself off the silly notion of including Las Vegas in your tour of the south-west, do so.) We drove down the main street and headed right on out of town. Death Valley was far more appealing.

The temperature on the road now was up to 130 degrees. We put wet clothes under our jackets and wrapped wet turbans around our heads. Driving for hours in such heat, even with interruptions for swims in tepid canyons, or for tinkering with a sick and overheated Harley, or for praying for your life as the bike lunges from side to side in the turbulent winds of mountain passes, has a debilitating effect on mind and body. It begins to bend you a little. It rakes at your flesh like claws. It passes out of the realms of mere scorching into some uncharted territory of pain. Camping out that night didn't appeal; I wanted crispy sheets and air-conditioning.

We pulled into a motel on the shores of Lake Mead—a tinpot joint with a bar and gaming room across the street which, like all bars in Nevada, contained perpetual night for the benefit of gamblers. We soaked for hours in hot water (high velocity grime takes weeks to shift), then turned the telly on to the local news. An atomic bomb had been tested 150 miles north that day. "What????" I was anxious enough about contracting cancer in this region, what with all the uranium tailings left on Indian reservations for the kids to play in, and what with actors dropping like flies because they'd been on location in this country, without having to contend with fallout.

After a sleepless night, during which I imagined I was being penetrated by deadly and invisible beams, we packed up at dawn. The cleaning lady arrived. I grabbed her arm and, with alarm in my voice, asked her if she'd heard the dreadful news. She smiled indulgently at this poor stupid foreigner and, with a certain pride, said, "Goodness, honey, there's nothin' to worry about. They go off all the time. Sometimes they're so big the walls shake. I think it affects the pot-plants a little, you know, but we're used to it around here . . . and it's better than being overrun by them I-ranians."

"Steve, get me out of here."

Death Valley. Second lowest point in the world. Weird moonscape mounds of borax, distorted by the heat mirage. (The temperature had climbed to 150.) Gold had been its original attraction, and the fever and madness that commodity has always inspired in the hearts of men led them to die in that desert in multitudes. Hence the name. There is nothing alive there.

The heat after 9 a.m. was impossible. The heat after 6 a.m. was impossible. We made a pact that we would travel on in the cooler hours, so when we called in at Furnace Springs—a truly glorious oasis with a pool and bar and groves of palms—we had several hours to fill in. Now, I had made certain rules at the beginning of this trip. One was never to travel over seventy miles per hour if it could possibly be avoided, another was never to drive after dark because Steve had next-to-no night vision, and the other was no booze. A cold beer here and there, okay, but no hard stuff. Steve found this one difficult, because his favourite hobby—after riding bikes—was getting drunk.

He had done well so far. But one drink led to another, and, while I swam in hot spring water, Stevie swam in cold beer. He didn't get drunk, mind you, just a wee bit unreliable. By the time we were ready to leave, the gas station had closed. We had to siphon petrol from a car. Stevie siphoned, and he siphoned and he siphoned. There was a small hole in the hose. He looked ill. He nearly passed out. He got rid of the nasty taste with yet more beer. "Steve, don't you think we'd better . . ." "I'm fine, Rob, jus' fine," he said, through a cheesy, cross-eyed grin. He chuckled and danced a perfectly straight line just to prove it.

It was dusk and down to 110 degrees. I didn't particularly want to get on the bike with him, but I didn't want to stay in Furnace Springs either. The first few miles were okay, then I noticed the white line doing curious twists under our wheels. Tap, tap, "Steve . . ." Tap, tap. "STEVE." "Huh?" "Stop the fucking bike." "What for?" as we narrowly missed the gravel at the side of the road. I began throttling him from the rear. A moon was rising over the nothingness. A scream was rising in my throat.

We camped that night beside the road, the hot wind moaning over us, the grit and borax sticking to our sweating bodies. It was nearly the Waterloo of a perfectly fine relationship. He wasn't even conscious of the kicks and oaths I planted on his snoring form. However, it is impossible to maintain such a level of passion during a Death Valley dawn, especially when you can see ice-tipped granite mountains about to pierce a sinking desert moon, as you travel up into California.

The first indication that we had crossed the border, besides the spinach salads with blue cheese dressing, was a west-coast denizen decked out in flapping multi-coloured paraphernalia passing us at a hundred miles an hour on his bike, with his feet up on the handlebars (I don't know how he managed it either), Walkman earphones clamped over his flying tresses, and a beer in his hand. Stevie's spirits were rising. He was recognising his roots.

California has deserts, mountains, lakes, San Francisco, oceans, Redwoods and oysters. Unfortunately it also has Californians. We spent a month there during which time Steve, in his search for the past, looked up many old acquaintances—who, he discovered, were either dead from heroin overdose and violence, or had changed from rabid pig-hating People's Park supporters to avid Ayn Rand aficionados. I think it almost broke him. Had we not stayed with his oldest friend Eric, I think he would have bitten more than one ghost from the past on the leg. But I shall come to Steve's tequila sunrise in due course.

There was now a certain urgency in our travels, which even California's lakes and mountain passes did little to pacify. By the time we reached Sacramento, tradesmen's entrance to the west coast, Stevie was like a bloodhound, hot on the trail of home. Back in New York he had casually let drop that because we rode a Harley we might end up fraternising with members of various bike groups along the way, and that I shouldn't worry, he would handle it. It wasn't that I had anything against the Hell's Angels or the Gypsy Jokers, but the thought of smiling wanly at forty toothless, tattooed, oil-soaked fourteen-stone brothers in the middle of nowhere and maybe blowing it was not my idea of fun. I had walked out of Mad Max. I knew about those guys. So when we called in at Sacramento to buy a new chain, and when the shopkeeper didn't have the tools for putting it on the bike, and when a toothless tattooed oil-soaked fourteen-stone brother kindly invited us back to his place so we could use his gear, and when Steve said okay despite my daggered looks which stuck six inches out his back, I died. I died.

We spent the afternoon at a little suburban house—Steve in the garage with twenty or so members of the Sacramento chapter, tinkering and talking about bikes, and me in the kitchen with our new friend's wife, talking about her kids, her husband and bikes. They completely dismantled my preconceptions about the Hell's Angels, but I'm glad we weren't black and riding a rice-burner.

On the crest of a windy hill that evening, we stopped to look at a finger of fog stretching across the Golden Gate Bridge into the bay, and rolling banks of it about to snuff out the lights of that lovely city: San Francisco—our destination. In Nevada we had bought the kinds of fireworks that were illegal in California, so we were warmly welcomed by Eric, a charming ex-pyromaniac who featured big in Steve's tall tales of sixties' insanity, who used to build cannons for a hobby and was now a jeweller, and who had mellowed a little with age and travel. Until we arrived. I noticed Eric's eyes glaze over and memory stir as he fingered the bottle rockets. The city was kept awake until the wee hours by overgrown, giggling five-year-olds and deafening explosions.

Despite such promising beginnings, despite hearing some of the greatest musicians in the world playing in small, intimate bars, despite making forays to the Santa Cruz Mystery Spot or watching seals frolic amongst the seaweed and rocks, the next two weeks brought about a perceptible decline in Steve's spirits.

Going home is traumatic enough after ten years, but when many of your old friends start quoting Reaganisms at you and saying "let 'em get a job" or "liberalism is dead," it's hard to remain cheerful, let alone diplomatic. It came to a head when we all headed north to a friend's place on the coast.

Eric forewarned Steve he would find the man changed, so, when we sat down to dinner in his fabulous restaurant that night, and when the chap suddenly, pugnaciously and without warning leant across the table, pointed his bobbing fork at Steve and said, "I suppose you think I've sold out, just because I worked my butt off for this restaurant? Well, I'm sick of feeling guilty and it's about time we Americans grew up and forgot all that crap about Vietnam and the welfare state—I mean, let 'em get a job. America has been the whipping boy for too long, and now it's time for good ol' American know-how to take us back to the top," Steve merely said, "Let's not argue; I think your restaurant's wonderful and good luck to you. The food's great."

"No, come on, man, I can see it in your eyes. As Ayn Rand says ..." The conversation was downhill from there on.

Back at his mansion it continued to plummet, as his wife chimed in with how the women's movement had been and gone in America, how it had worked, and was now just a lot of screwed-up dykes causing trouble. We all drank too much, which never helps. I eventually went to bed, unable to bear the strain of smiling through clenched teeth. Stevie had that dangerously belligerent light in his eyes so, when he came in to say goodnight and told me that if his friend didn't stop looking for an argument he'd have to worry him round the ankles like a bulldog, I knew there'd be trouble.

Eric carried him into the bedroom at seven in the morning— an incident with a crossbow, a run-in with a woodpile, and three bottles of tequila later. I lay next to his unconscious form as long as I decently could, but eventually had to get up and socialise with the offended couple. I had to, with the help of the wonderful Eric, smooth the troubled waters until three in the afternoon, when a sickly, cross-eyed, tequila-sodden wreck staggered out of the bed-room, farted, said thanks for the lovely evening, and left on his Harley with me on the back saying yes, lovely, do hope we see you again, do hope your ankles heal soon and sorry about the crossbow, ha ha. We nursed our hangovers in the giant Redwoods.

A week later I took a Harley and a shell-shocked friend back to Australia. Whatever lingering doubts he had had about wanting to live in his home-country were cured forever. As for me, the only permanent injuries I sustained from the journey are a small, numb patch on my bottom and a cemented trepidation about current American thinking.

I wanted to end this piece saying something positive, apprecia-tive and lyrical about Australia's Big Brother, wanted to convince myself that all the wonderful people we met there and all my expatriate Yank buddies and all the good thought that comes out of there make up for the born-again nuke 'em mentality that pervades the place. But for the life of me I couldn't do it. Except, of course, that it's a hell of a nice place to visit.

Ellesmere: Two Men Alone in a World of Ice

Jon Turk

Editors' note: Jon Turk received his PhD in chemistry in 1971 and wrote the first environmental science textbook in North America, but left academia to engage in extreme expeditions in remote parts of the world. Jon's two-year kayak passage across the North Pacific Rim was named by Paddler *magazine as one of the ten greatest sea kayaking expeditions of all time. His circumnavigation of Ellesmere with Erik Boomer was nominated by* National Geographic *as one of the top ten adventures of 2011. It was also awarded "Expedition of the Year" by* Canoe & Kayak *magazine in 2011, was reported on the front page of the* New York Times *in 2012, and received first place in print journalism at the 2013 Northern Lights Awards. Jon chronicles his journeys and mental and spiritual passages in a trilogy of three books:* Cold Oceans, *about the mind-set of expedition success;* In the Wake of the Jomon, *about kayaking across the Pacific Ocean; and* The Raven's Gift, *which chronicles the teachings of one of the last Siberian shamans who was born into a Stone Age existence. Here he describes the first circumnavigation of Ellesmere Island in a kayak.*

An ice floe the size of a football field drifted slowly toward the cliff, rotated, and buckled. The air filled with a human-like groan, followed by a sharp crack that echoed off the nearby mountain. Ice crystals exploded and danced rainbows in the sunshine, while

10-foot thick chunks rose 30 feet out of the sea and smeared against solid rock.

Boomer and I were trapped.

An ocean current was driving the North Pole ice pack into the Robeson Channel, a 12-mile wide constriction between Ellesmere Island and the northern coast of Greenland. Behind this floe, a seemingly infinite reservoir of polar ice was moving southward under compression of tectonic magnitude. Our path was blocked.

We were an odd couple to contemplate spending eternity together. Erik Boomer is 40 years younger than me, closer in age to my grandchildren than to my children. He is a world-class whitewater paddler, who before this expedition had never sat in a sea kayak. I was 65 years old, and though I hadn't paddled a Class V river in a number of years, I'd rounded Cape Horn and crossed the North Pacific in a sea kayak.

Despite, or perhaps because of our differences, we had already traveled 750 miles across the Arctic icepack, dragging our loaded kayaks over the snow and tortured ice, wading through meltwater pools, and occasionally crawling in heavy slush and ice. We had learned to work together and rely on one another. We were a team now, and we both felt it deep down, where it counts.

We were in this predicament together: Between our two little selves and the first outpost of civilization lay more than 750 miles of hard travel. We had food for days, and for 17 days we had gone nowhere. We were trapped. If we ventured into dangerous ice, we could be crushed. But if we waited for optimal conditions, we could sit here until our food was gone and winter descended. In order to survive, we needed to find that razor thin edge between boldness and caution.

❧

Bill Bradt is an old river-running buddy. When his son Tyler was 6 or 7 years old, we sat him in a kayak and launched down the West

Fork of the Bitterroot, near our homes in Western Montana. He looked so tiny in that cockpit, elbows raised so he could dip his paddle in the water. Over the years, I watched Tyler grow into that kayak. Then suddenly, it seemed, as Bill and I became progressively older and slower, Tyler was testing his extraordinary talent on the most difficult whitewater on the planet, including a record-setting plunge over 186-foot Palouse Falls in 2009.

Then, one day, an email popped up. "Hey, maybe we should do an expedition together?"

Age was creeping up. Sixty-five feels significantly older than 60. Yet I had one big expedition dream left to fulfill: a 1,500-mile circumnavigation of Ellesmere Island by ski and sea kayak. I'd thought about it since 1988, when Chris Seashore and I had paddled from Ellesmere to Greenland. The towering glaciers, moving ice, and stark exposure of that vast and uninhabited seascape had captured my imagination. Incredibly, no one had attempted the circumnavigation, one of the last great prizes in the Arctic. Tyler and I agreed to attempt it together.

We would use two food drops and carry provisions for 100 days, meaning that we'd need to average 15 miles—half a marathon—every day for more than three months. Experienced polar explorers warned us that rough ice on the North Coast would slow our passage to a mile a day, or a few hundred yards, or nothing at all. And once the ice broke up in late summer, we would be paddling overloaded boats through open water exposed to Arctic storms. Over coffee in Duluth, Lonnie Dupre, who had circumnavigated Greenland in 2001, advised me that our bodies would simply not withstand the torture of 100 continuous days. We'd need to rest along the way, he said. We wouldn't have enough food or time to rest, yet for no rational reason, the circumnavigation still seemed possible to us.

The advice did convince us to add more muscle to our team. Tyler suggested Erik Boomer, a whitewater charger revered for his physical strength and clear-headed optimism. When we described the trip's many challenges and the experts' warnings, Boomer smiled casually as if we were discussing a trade run of a local river. "Sure," he said. "I'm in."

Eddie Bauer–First Ascent became our major sponsor and we won a Polartec Grant. Wilderness Systems provided boats, and AT donated paddles. Then, on March 21, less than six weeks before our planned departure, another email popped up. It was from Tyler, and the subject line read "Bad News."

"Hi guys, I really fucked up. My boat flattened out halfway down a big falls and I broke my back. I'll know a lot more in the morning when I talk to the neurosurgeon."

Tyler would eventually make a full recovery, but if Boomer and I were to attempt the Ellesmere circumnavigation, it would be without Tyler. He was the force holding us together, the apex of our human triangle. Now Boomer and I were two strangers, 40 years apart, preparing to travel together in total isolation, for more than three months, with the assurance that we would face life-and-death decisions.

Many people have insisted that I must have had reservations about traveling so far and so long with a stranger, a generation younger than me. We had no music, no books, no playing cards, just eight rumpled, torn out pages of the Tao Te Ching. What would we talk about? How would we resolve differences in the face of tense situations? We had plenty to worry about in the days before flying north, but I always trusted Boomer. Previously, I had kayaked 3,000 miles across the North Pacific Rim with Misha Petrov, a Russian who had never been in a kayak before. I think you can trust a person by recognizing the madness that propels them, and in Boomer's madness I saw my own.

In 1971, I had stuffed my Ph.D. diploma in the glove box of a ratty old Ford Fairlane, lashed a canoe on top, and headed into the Arctic. Boomer had also experimented with possessions and jobs. He put them aside to go North and run the Stikine, and the Susitna, and Turnback Canyon on the Alsek. We'd miss Tyler's magnetic personality and booming laugh, but an even stronger thread would hold Boomer and me together—the mischievous grin of the Arctic wilderness.

Boomer and I set off on May 7 from Grise Fiord, the northernmost hamlet in Canada and the only civilian settlement on the island. This would be my retirement party—one last journey into a world that had shaped my life since I dropped out of research chemistry 40 years ago. Boomer was seeking a new vision of adventure, expanded from his already formidable accomplishments as a world-class whitewater boater.

The temperature was in the mid teens when we skied out of town, pulling our kayaks as sleds across a frozen ocean. We were carrying 25 days of food, and our total loads, including the boats, weighed 225 pounds. Everything was a compromise because every piece of gear, from kayaks to underwear, had to function in three radically different environments—winter on dry snow; break up and slush; and open water Arctic paddling. The Wilderness Systems Tsunami 135, advertised on the company website as "ideal for female and small-framed paddlers," was clearly smaller than we would have liked, but it was the largest boat that fit into the airplane that flies to Grise.

The first leg of the journey was 400 miles to the Canadian weather station at Eureka, on the west coast of the island. In the frenzy of preparation, I'd glued and screwed my skins on backwards so now I hobbled along like a skateboarder with square wheels. Boomer's boots didn't fit well and after a few days he constructed new footwear out of silver tape and scraps of shoe-like material he scavenged from an outlying hunting cabin.

The temperature dropped to below zero, and the north wind blew the snow into rock-hard drifts. We pulled our hoods tight against frozen faces and trudged past polar bear tracks and herds of muskoxen. One day we disagreed on whether to take a short cut overland, and on another day we argued about whether we should take a shortcut across the sea ice. But, very quickly, we learned to trust each other. It wasn't a verbalized emotion, but like the eight water-stained pages of the Tao, it just was. And anyway, as the Tao teachers reminded us, no one knew the answers to the most pressing questions, such as, "How far can we push our bodies today, and still travel every day for three and a half months?" "How many miles can we maintain on will-power alone, and when do we tickle the dragon of basic metabolic limitations?" We had no idea, at the start, how perilously close we would come to answering that question.

We resupplied at Eureka weather station, which is distinguished for having the lowest average annual temperature of any weather station in Canada. It squatted on a hillside like a space ship out of time: gleaming stainless steel kitchens, hot water, internet, and television. We rested for a day and a half and packed for the next leg of our expedition, to a food cache on the North Coast, 350 miles away.

We'd been travelling on the west coast of Ellesmere, in the lee of nearby Axel Heiberg Island. Protected from the currents and waves of the open ocean, the sea ice here forms a relatively smooth surface, making travel easy. In contrast, the North Coast is exposed to the continuously churning, moving, colliding, North Polar ice pack. We heard reports of nearly impenetrable pressure ridges, formed from colliding multi-year ice.

So, did we need food for 20 days, or 50? Or was the passage impossible? Should we turn back and abort the mission at the first encounter with rough ice? Or push on into the mayhem, risking the unpleasant possibility of starving to death in the middle of it—unable to move forward, and too far along to retreat?

The line between courage and foolishness is drawn only after the fat lady sings. If you make it, you were courageous. If you die, all the Monday morning quarterbacks can puff up their chests and call you a fool. We set off with 50 days of food, which was as much as we could carry, mandating that we average seven miles a day.

All along the northwest coast, Boomer and I found magic passages through potentially jagged ice. On many headlands, mini glaciers flowed into the sea, providing smooth snow and seamless travel over land. Thus, we continued onward into the summer solstice, feeling lucky and clever, yet always apprehensive that tomorrow would be the day that our path was blocked.

The miles passed underfoot, but they didn't come easy. Our feet became blistered and swollen, and our bodies ached. Every day, by late afternoon, my brain was too tired to process the input from my eyes, so I saw double and blurry. I relied on Boomer's younger vision and incredible strength to find routes through the ice.

By mid-June, the summer sun had melted the previous season's snow cover, revealing sharp chunks of pressure ridge ice. Boomer's skis broke. He moved his bindings and pushed ahead on the stubs. In this way we crossed the 350 miles in 22 days, found our cache, and celebrated with Pringles and rum. Now loaded to 300 pounds, we set out again, still dragging our boats. Near Cape Hecla, we finally encountered the feared maze of pressure ridges. Rock cliffs lined the shore and the sea had metamorphosed into a kaleidoscope of jagged ice, deep slush, and frigid freshwater lakes that pooled on the surface. We walked, paddled, or pushed along with ski poles through the meltwater pools, helped each other over the steepest ice, and crawled across the slush on hands and knees because we couldn't get enough traction using just our feet. When you're soaking wet and crawling across super-saturated snow, it doesn't do any good to remind yourself that you still have 800 miles to go.

On the afternoon of July 4th, we rounded the northeast corner of Ellesmere into the Robeson Channel. Here, the sun and current had fractured the ice into independently moving floes. Some were many acres in size, while others were as large as a house, or a tent, or a baseball. A current was driving ice from the North Polar Sea southward, into the narrow constriction between Ellesmere and Greenland. As a result, all the floes were compressed together, churning, spinning, and threatening to crush anything in their path.

We climbed to a rocky headland and watched the ice parade along the coast, imagining the despair that turn-of-the-century explorers must have felt as their stout wooden ships were crushed in the mayhem. We discussed the unpleasant option of walking to Grise Fiord, overland and half starved, after the ocean froze again in the fall. But when we tried to imagine a route over the mountains, with no climbing gear and not even adequate backpacks, we realized that it was impossible. We had to get through the ice.

The days ticked by. Occasionally, we made a mile, or two, or three. For nine days we sat in our tent, going nowhere. Every day the sun settled lower in the sky, reminding us that even though we still enjoyed 24 hour daylight, winter would soon descend upon us with Polar speed and ferocity. Our food supply dwindled. Boldness or caution? Caution or boldness? Too much of either would kill us. We sat on the shore and watched the parade of ice. Think out of the box. There must be a way. Finally, we convinced ourselves to risk a treacherous passage across moving ice onto one of the large floes. Our theory was that if we chose a floe strong enough to withstand collisions with the rest of the ice, we could ride it southward with the current.

On July 13th, a large floe, about 5 to 10 acres in size and consisting of thick, multiyear ice, floated to within 400 yards of shore. We reasoned that this floe would survive the ravages of continuous collisions and provide a safe "ship" to carry us south. The current slowed at slack tide, giving us a narrow time window to cross from shore to the floe. The intervening distance was choked with small pieces of ice floating in a watery matrix. Some of this ice was large and stable enough to stand on, but other floes were small and tippy. We attached a long line to the boats and jumped from one unstable fragment of ice to another, until we reached the safety of the first large chunk. Then we pulled the boats across to join us. But now our continued passage was blocked by a small open channel wider than we dared jump across. So, Boomer bridged the gap with his kayak and crawled across the deck, in a gymnastic tightrope act. I followed. Next, we seal-launched into an even wider passage, paddled a few boat lengths, and climbed out of the boats and back onto the ice. Moving in this eclectic manner, we traveled a quarter of a mile in three hours.

Once we reached the large floe, we high fived, and set up our tent in the warm sunshine. We were determined to stay aboard this enormous ice shard for a week or more, if necessary, through all changes in tide and weather, as it carried us effortlessly toward Grise Fiord. Initially our GPS told us that we were heading south at 0.3 to 0.4 knots. That's not much, but if sustained, it would multiply to 4–5 miles a day, which is significantly faster than nothing. Boomer stood on a pressure ridge and held an imaginary steering wheel in his hand, grinning with joy and pretending he was the captain of a massive diesel-munching ice breaker.

At the next slack tide, the floe stopped, and then, in the middle of the night, began drifting north with the ebb at 1 knot. We were traveling the wrong way at more than twice the speed of our earlier southward passage. The ice compression relaxed and open water stretched all around us. Then, the ice started squeezing together again. I couldn't tell whether we were drifting north and the ice to the north of us was stationary, or if we were stationary and the ice to the north was crashing into us. In any case, in the semi twilight of the Arctic night, the surrounding water became smaller and smaller as if it were being sucked into a black hole. The collision occurred with a slushy, wooshy sound, not a metallic clang. The edges of our floe crumpled and fractured, shooting ice splinters into the air, while the center, where we were huddled together in fear and awe, rippled, as if it were impacted by an earthquake. There is no metaphor to describe what was happening. This wasn't like anything. It was the Arctic icepack compressing and fracturing into rubble.

At the next slack water, we reversed our tenuous and terrifying passage across small floes and returned to terra firma, having traveled a net distance of one mile away from our goal.

For the next week, we inched southward, averaging about 1,200 yards a day. In places where the shoreline was still covered with winter snowdrifts, we dragged overland. Occasionally we paddled short distances between giant pressure ridges, and once we portaged over talus and rock. Several days we waited, going nowhere. Finally we reached a zone where steep cliffs dropped sharply into the sea. We could no longer travel a mile or two and return safely to land. If we were caught in the strait when the ice closed in on us, we would be crushed within unimaginable forces.

A good friend, Paul Attalla, had advised us, "Be patient. Don't do anything stupid." We broke our bags apart, counted our food, and then grimly packed everything up again. Don't do anything stupid? Fine. It would be stupid to paddle into the ice and get crushed, and equally stupid to wait and starve.

We needed a south wind to push the ice out of the way, and hold it clear for the five hours it would take us to race past the cliffs and reach the next safe landing. On the morning of July 21st, the compression seemed to be easing up, and we had a weather report of favorable wind. We paddled into narrow channels between the floes. A 20-foot iceberg collapsed moments after I paddled past it. "OK, no worries," I told myself. "Nothing bad actually happened." But I couldn't stop worrying any more than I could stop breathing.

In whitewater, the current is flowing, but at least the rocks stay still. Here, everything was moving, so there was no stable reality.

Our open-water channel slammed shut, so we dragged our boats onto a large floe, and started hiking toward the south edge, where a remnant of open water remained. Boomer was ahead and urged me to move faster, but I was going all out. There was no "faster" left inside me. No, this wasn't right. We couldn't continue if our survival constantly depended on split-second timing.

We traveled another mile, until just offshore of Cape Union, fear overpowered desperation. Reluctantly, we retraced our tenuous steps to our old camp, elated to be unscathed.

We slept to let the adrenaline drain away. When we woke, even more open water presented itself, so we paddled out for a second time that day. But after about half a mile, we got scared again and retreated. Discouraged, we pitched the tent and ate dinner. It seemed as if we would never leave this place. After all, when Adolphus Greely set up camp to the south of us in 1881, he was isolated for three years before a resupply ship could break through. Nineteen of the original 25 men died of starvation, drowning, hyperthermia, and, in one case, firing squad. Greely ordered the man shot for stealing food, after which his comrades may have eaten him (no one knows for sure). I wanted to close my eyes and stop thinking about our predicament, but Boomer took one last scouting mission to watch the ice. He returned breathlessly.

"Looks good out there. I think we can go for it."

For the third time that day, we paddled southward toward the rock-bound coastline. The summer sun had swung into the northern sky to cast a subdued grayness across the seascape, offset by the soft white glow of the ice. We were already exhausted from our previous two ordeals, but this is the moment you live for as an adventurer. It is comparable to pulling out of an eddy into a big rapid, or turning skis into the fall line and dropping into a steep, snaking couloir. It is the moment when you must trust yourself and your partner absolutely and completely. A trust earned by traveling across the Arctic, alone together. It is the glorious moment when fear vaporizes because you have decided to commit, and fear is now a needless distraction.

A major league baseball player reaches the Hall of Fame if he connects once out of every three times at bat. An NBA basketball player draws a multimillion dollar salary if he hits 50 percent. An adventurer must have a lifetime batting average of 1,000. Nothing less. I had a gut feeling that we would make it that night, but don't remind me how much we were depending on blind luck.

It was July 21. For us it was the first day of summer because, after 76 days, it was the first time we paddled our kayaks as if we were on a sea kayak expedition. And, in true Arctic fashion, it was the first day of winter as well, because in the wee hours of the morning, as we were battling the fatigue of an all-night ordeal, a thin film of ice formed on the sea, emitting a tinkling sound as we dipped our paddles and moved southward, toward home.

As July slowly morphed into August, the sea ice was fractured, moving, and sometimes thick, but not impenetrable. Most days, we paddled in narrow channels through an infinite maze of glistening floes. Occasionally the floes compressed together and blocked our passage, but after the Robeson Channel, these compressions were short lived. When we could go no farther, we hauled out on land, or onto a large floe, and waited for a change in tide or wind. Sometimes we dragged on the closely packed ice, jumping across small tippy floes.

One day, Boomer was attacked by a walrus—a ton and a half of awkwardly graceful skin, blubber and muscle, its gleaming ivory tusks rearing above Boomer's head. Or maybe he wasn't attacked after all; maybe the walrus was just curious, getting a better look. In any case, whack, whack, Boomer smacked the monster in the face and paddled away ferociously. On another day, a polar bear slobbered over the vestibule and gently bit a small hole in our tent. Was he attacking, or like the walrus, just visiting in his polar bear way? We'll never know, but we do know that the Arctic and its creatures showed us their power, and then turned their gentle side to grant us safe passage.

Boomer and I paddled into Grise Fiord on August 19th, after 104 days and 1,500 miles. We celebrated by sautéing up some potatoes, cabbage, and onions, and binging on chips and salsa. Then, 39 hours after arriving in town, I woke in the night and discovered that I couldn't pee. It's a body function that you normally take for granted, like heartbeat or digestion. But when it failed, my blood pressure and potassium levels shot sky high. The nurse at the local clinic listed my condition as "life threatening." Pilots from Global Rescue flew their jet through a fast-closing weather window to carry me south. They saved my life.

Now I am safely home in the mountains of Western Montana. My urologist tells me that it was merely a coincidence that my system shut down immediately after the expedition was complete. But endurance athletes, trainers, and naturopathic doctors tell me that in that wonderland of sea and ice, my body was on the brink of collapse and the brain said, "Not yet, old friend. We're in this together, you and me, brain and urinary tract. Hang on. You can shut down after we get to town."

There's no way to know. But I can tell you that out there, surrounded by walrus, storms, polar bears and ice, I felt a cathartic oneness of all things, animate and inanimate. If it were somehow possible to internalize the essence of a landscape into one's being, I would become the Ellesmere coastline.

Walking on the Mountains
of the Moon

Cameron M. Burns

Editors' note: Cameron M. Burns has traveled the world and climbed new routes and peaks in dozens of countries. He is the author of many books on adventure and travel, including the first ice-climbing guide to Colorado and the first guidebook to California's 14,000-foot mountains (with coauthor Steve Porcella). He grew up in the northern outskirts of Sydney and spent many years adventuring in the bush around his boyhood home—when he wasn't surfing. Here he describes his first trip to the Rwenzori Mountains in Uganda.

If someone were to quiz you on what you thought was the most exotic mountain range on earth, you might suggest some unexplored alpine chain in Asia or South America. You might suggest a huge desert uplift in, say, Oman or Jordan. You might even suggest an urban "range," like the crags of Hong Kong or Sydney. I'd put forth the Rwenzoris in Africa, a range of mountains so geographically, topographically, and climatically unique that they defy every notion of Africa you've ever had.

They are wet—so moist that Scottish missionary David Livingstone didn't realize they existed (although he lived just a few miles away for twelve years) because they were permanently immersed in cloud. They are tall, for Africa, with the higher peaks reaching nearly 17,000 feet. They have glaciers and jungles, often only a few feet apart. They boast virgin summits and massive unclimbed walls. Their lower slopes are roamed by both noisy chimpanzees and machine gun–toting guerrillas. And their very existence was a huge puzzle that took more than two thousand years to figure out.

I was lucky enough to visit the Rwenzoris (pronounced Roo-wen-zorees) in 2006 as part of a guidebook-updating trip. I figured the new edition should include the standard routes on the three highest Rwenzori peaks (Mounts Stanley, Speke, and Baker). The routes are quasi-technical walk-ups (you want to be roped up crossing the glaciers), to be sure, but my real goal was to explore the range for future climbing possibilities.

With a couple of friends well versed in African travel, I set off for Uganda. We were about to have a few issues of our own.

When you hit the ground in Uganda, an overwhelming sense of desperation overcomes you. Like most visitors, we flew into Entebbe and caught a taxi into Kampala, Uganda's compact capital and the home of tribal and colonial rulers for centuries. The streets were filled with broken buses, overloaded public minibuses, scooters carrying four people (and furniture), skinny bullocks tugging ratty carts, and a red dust that swirled upward everyplace that was unpaved. Most people did not look happy. The poverty was obvious and extreme, and we passed dozens of vehicles driven by foreign-aid workers, some supplying food and medical supplies, others with clothing and educational materials, many with bibles. Most vehicles, sadly, carried United Nations peacekeeping forces, headed for the northern part of the country and battle, literally, with the brutal Lord's Resistance Army (LRA).

Before leaving home, Benny Bach, Charlie French, and I had studied the LRA and BBC reports of the atrocities being carried out along the Uganda-Sudan border. We'd also pored over news reports about troop buildups in the Democratic Republic of Congo to Uganda's west. (A 1996 war in the DRC, which showed signs of re-erupting daily, had ultimately involved nine other African nations, and the DRC had, as one BBC reporter wrote, the "potential to drag down the prospects of the whole continent"). Wide-eyed, we'd read reports about Ugandan crime, AIDS, the failing infrastructure, the bad roads, and diseases. Worse still were the older reports, from the late 1990s, about the butchering of eight "gorilla tourists" (Americans, Brits, and Kiwis) in Uganda's Bwindi Impenetrable National Park by a guy who used the moniker "Van Damme," and a report about Ugandan army officers who fought a pitched battle with Rwandan Hutu extremists in a national park on the eastern side of the DRC.

Worst of all, though, were the vague reports that rebels fighting the Ugandan government—known as the Allied Democratic Forces (ADF)—might once again be using the Rwenzoris, the famed Mountains of the Moon, as a staging ground for attacks on the Ugandan army.

Clearly, a range of issues.

As the taxi climbed into the hill district of Kampala, a huge black cloud descended over the city, the taxi, and us, and a monsoon-like rain began to pummel everyone and everything. The ghost of former dictator Idi Amin was hosting a celestial welcoming party.

The cleansing wash wasn't just symbolic. Water is at the heart of the folklore, legends, and economy of the Rwenzoris, and it's why they're famous.

In the ancient world, centered around the "sea at the center of the earth" (the Mediterranean), scholars knew of the Nile River's existence, but its massive output of freshwater flowing through the desert was a paradox. Where did it come from? Why was it so big? The origin of the Nile was a vast riddle.

By most accounts, the first geographer to assemble a notion of mountains as the river's source was the Greek philosopher Claudius Ptolemy, who in about AD 150 wrote of the "Lunae Montes," or Mountains of the Moon. But Ptolemy had many predecessors, starting with Aeschylus, who in 500 BC wrote of "Egypt nurtured by the snows." Aeschylus was followed by Herodotus, who in 450 BC described a spring fed by the waters of a bottomless lake located between two steep peaks, Crophi and Mophi, and then Aristotle, who in 350 BC wrote of a "silver mountain" as the source of the Nile.

"There has been much dispute among geographers as to whether these early references applied to the Rwenzori, the Virunga Mountains, the country of Banyamwenzi [people of the moon], Mount Kenya and Kilimanjaro, or Ethiopia," wrote Henry Osmaston and David Pasteur, British mountaineers who in 1972 produced the superb *Guide to the Rwenzori*. "There is evidence for the last, but the problem is probably insoluble and now the Rwenzori have, by superior publicity, firmly established their claim to be at least the modern Mountains of the Moon."

There is little recorded history between the time of the ancients and the better-documented period of British exploration of East Africa, which occurred, for the most part, in the nineteenth century. Between the 1840s and the end of that century, explorers such as Baker, Burton, Speke, Livingstone, and Stanley plied the savannah from Mombasa to the Rift Valley in search of the Nile's headwaters. They learned, eventually, that the various mountain ranges and East Africa's Great Lakes all contributed to the Nile.

Specifically, it was Henry Morton Stanley—originally sent to Africa to find Livingstone and who uttered exploration's most memorable phrase, "Dr. Livingstone, I presume?"—who realized there were mountains in the ever-looming clouds that boiled up over western Uganda from the Congo Basin. In 1888, in the middle of an attempt to rescue a colonial ruler in western Uganda, Stanley was crossing the southwestern edge of Lake Albert when he beheld the snowcapped Rwenzoris, making him likely the first European to recognize the range as, well, a range.

The origin of the colorful name "Mountains of the Moon" is unclear, but Ptolemy used it as far back as AD 150. Thankfully, the word Rwenzori (not Ruwenzori) itself has a simpler origin: According to Osmaston, it was made up by Stanley, who used several names given to the mountains by the area's tribes.

As my traveling companions, Benny and Charlie, and I learned on our first day, these are wet mountains. The Rwenzoris are nearly always covered in cloud. The average rainfall is roughly 98 inches a year, according to the United Nations. Their valleys are steep, and the valley bottoms are clogged with mud, many feet deep. The foliage is surreal, with giant lobelias and groundsels dominating the forest, and massive, nearly impenetrable tangles of ground cover. Weirdly, though, the plants remain incredibly dry, and the local Bakonjo porters can start a fire using even the most sodden wood, anytime they must.

On arrival in the tiny village of Nyakalengija, where most of the officially required porters and guides live, we quickly found our excursion would be more than just a horticultural experience. After a short briefing on the flora, fauna, and rules of the park, Josiah Makwano, a cheery, round-faced Bakonjo ranger, slung his machine gun over his arm and explained he was coming along—to protect us.

Compared to the highly regulated treadmill on Kilimanjaro (up to 28,000 trekkers and climbers injecting millions of dollars into northern Tanzania's economy), the Rwenzoris are still an East African frontier. Ironically, the infamous Idi Amin did a favor for mountaineers heading to the Rwenzoris by turning the whole world off. That's why some Rwenzori peaks remain, or seem to remain, unclimbed.

Our plan was pretty simple: wander up the big three (Mounts Stanley, Speke, and Baker), then do a little "wildcatting," as Benny likes to call it—exploring new ground. Prior to the trip, we had pored over books on the Rwenzoris and examined the remote valleys on the southern edge of the range. One peak, Keki ("Cake-ee"), grabbed our attention because, as Osmaston and Pasteur wrote:

"13,500 feet . . . this appears to be steep-sided and may be difficult to climb. No ascent has been recorded." Later, in a book from the 1930s, we found a watercolor painting of Keki, and it looked a lot like Hallett Peak in our own Rocky Mountain National Park: steep-walled and likely fun to climb.

Andrew Wielochowski's map of the Rwenzoris had Keki marked, too, but the way to get to the mountain seemed anything but straightforward. Also, the more maps we looked at, the more we realized that this portion of the range was something of an unknown, a black hole in mountain geography. We soon labeled our lack of information the "Keki Hole." We managed to reach Henry Osmaston, however, and thirty-two years after the publication of his book, he told us via e-mail that, indeed, the plum cake–shaped hunk of land was, as far as he knew, still unclimbed. We had a mission.

Our first week was spent trudging up the standard trekking routes on the main summits. Sadly, though, before even our first peak, Mount Speke, one of our guides, Eric Baluku, suffered a debilitating bout of malaria and had to be sent home. Many Westerners—acutely aware of the well-publicized effect of AIDS on Africans—seem to forget about malaria, another one of Africa's biggest killers. According to the World Health Organization, "There are at least 300 million acute cases of malaria each year globally, resulting in more than a million deaths. Around 90 percent of these deaths occur in Africa, mostly in young children." All the East Africans I've met have had relatives die from it, and according to several knowledgeable Bakonjos, most of the Rwenzori guides and porters suffer from it. Eric was replaced a few days later by a small, smiling chap named Fred Bosco.

We wandered over Mount Speke from east to west—a trip another one of our guides, a Catholic priest named Peter Babughagle, had done in the 1970s—to learn that the huge glacier that existed thirty years ago on Speke's east side was now completely gone. Peter, who hadn't been up there in a decade, was in total disbelief. Two days later we wandered up Mount Stanley, to the highest point in the range, Margherita (5,109 meters), as the glaciers underfoot flowed with melting ice.

Like mountains around the globe, especially those on the equator, the Rwenzoris are melting out as a result of global warming. Before the regional turmoil of the 1990s, scientists had repeatedly ventured into the Rwenzoris to examine glacial retreat and had come away with shocking discoveries about equatorial ice fields. In 1990 a group of Austrian researchers found the Rwenzori glaciers had been retreating at about 12 meters per year for the previous two decades. In June 2003, after the region had become relatively safe again, British geographer Richard Taylor led a team that surveyed the ice on Mounts Stanley and Speke, and learned that the Elena Glacier had retreated about 140 meters since 1990, while the Speke Glacier had retreated 311 meters in the same period. (Glaciologists have for a long time painted rocks at the glaciers' snouts to measure the retreat.) Taylor's team concluded in its report that "snow will disappear from the Rwenzori mountains in the next two to three decades and possibly by the year 2023."

My strongest memory of the Elena Glacier is the distraught look on Charlie's face as we stood on the pockmarked and dirty ice sheet, which was covered with half an inch of water, all of it draining quickly downhill.

We wandered up Mount Baker a couple of days later and then, finally, had a chance to give back, or at least try. Charlie had spent half our sole rest day staring at a pretty slab opposite the Kitandara Hut in the middle of the range, and he suggested it needed climbing—not just by us, but by the whole crew: some twelve porters (at that point) and the guides themselves. We set up a toprope.

Reaching summits is a fine reward in the mountaineering world, whatever the route, whatever the difficulty, and regardless of the suffering. But teaching folks to climb in an exotic region of the world—one that will surely see more and more visitors and where rock-climbing skills are virtually unknown—was the highlight of our journey.

The next day we set off, into the unknown, the Keki Hole. It was time to disappear down one of the unfrequented Rwenzori valleys and play Stanley and Livingstone.

By this point, about ten days into our jaunt, the local guides and porters had become trusted friends. We were sharing meals and gear, and they had even sent one porter out to their village, Nyakalengija, to get us gumboots for walking. The deep layer of mud and moss and the wild steepness of the Rwenzori valleys combine to make usually simple foot-travel a serious undertaking. Indeed, after leaving Kitandara Hut, it took us a full day to cover a couple of kilometers on the nonexistent "trail" (well marked on the maps, of course). The gumboots, though, stuck to rock as well as any climbing boots do, and we soon had the entire crew of Ugandans out bouldering in the forest.

After cresting Bamwanjara Pass, we entered the upper Kamusongi River valley and, at last, found Keki. Predictably, it was a miserable little turd. There was naught we could do except scramble up the dirty hummock where, on top, we found a thirty-year-old cairn. Our new peak was a bust.

We continued down the valley to catch our final pickup at the southeastern edge of the mountains in a small mining town called Kilembe. We stumbled on through the mud, lamenting our shoddy research.

A few kilometers later, the topography began to change. The valleys became steeper, and the rock walls skirting them got taller and taller. By nightfall, at a rock shelter called Mutinda, we found ourselves sitting under a cluster of rock towers and walls that were a cross between Venezuelan tepuis and Costa Rican highlands. The next day we clawed our way up grass humps and sideways trees and bagged an elegant-looking spire, where the low-fifth-class climbing was made significantly harder by huge sheets of moss that peeled off when we mantled onto ledges. (We rated the route M2, from the moss-climbing rating system.) It was February 11, my first daughter's birthday, so we dubbed the peak Zoe's Needle and descended. Halfway down, I decided to try another nearby summit. After all, I have two little girls, and when birthdays come along they both get something, no matter how silly.

While Benny and Peter Babughagle headed back to camp, Charlie and I attempted a summit similar to Zoe's Needle. We ditched the rock gear, expecting low-fifth-class rock at the most, and were soon soloing up a dirty chimney with much harder climbing than expected. Charlie backed off, but our second "guide," Fred, soloed the chimney behind me—eyes as wide as platters. We built a cairn on the summit, downclimbed the chimney, and descended to camp. Mollie's Tower was in the bag.

Naming the summits of these mountains after monarchs was a trend started by the Duke of Abruzzi in 1906, when he named Margherita, Alexandra, Elizabeth, and a dozen other summits. I figured we were continuing the tradition; Princesses Zoe and Mollie, when I called them via satellite phone, were most excited, though a bit uncertain of what Africa was (and probably who I was—I'm never sure of that myself). We continued out to Kilembe.

In all, it was a modest excursion, but it opened our eyes to the possibilities tucked away on the edge of the great Congo Basin.

Back in the village of Nyakalengija, we held something of a going-away party, at which we handed out tips and thanked our crew of locals. It was a sad farewell. Over the course of fifteen days, three *abbajungus* from the West had grown tight with eighteen Bakonjos they'd never met before—and they seemed to think we were okay, too, cash or no cash.

Mountain enthusiasts are often labeled selfish and egotistical, but in places like Uganda, climbers (and trekkers) represent the front line of economic development and, often, stability. Between

July and December 2001, there were 118 foreign visitors to the Rwenzoris, according to park statistics. In the dry season of the northern winter (January, February, etc.) of 2005, there were hundreds and hundreds of foreign visitors—mostly trekkers, but a few climbers as well. And the Ugandan government is planning to foster tourism. As Lilliame Nakanagi, from the office of the advisor to the president of Uganda, told me in a chance meeting in Kampala, "It's extremely important that foreign travelers know they can be safe here."

According to park officials, we had prompted the reestablishment of a route through the mountains' southern section, something they had longed to do for years—to offer visitors more trekking options and to inject some cash into a village (Kilembe) subject to the fits and starts of a mining economy.

As for the more global issue of climate change, we all have to work on it. I've long believed energy policy is not just a federal or international matter, but a state, local, and even family issue. After our 2005 Rwenzori excursion, I returned home and in four hours of web-clicking was able to switch my family's electricity supply to full wind power. I also installed compact fluorescent lightbulbs in sockets that didn't already have them, applied to my homeowners' association to put up solar panels, and signed up my family as the first family entity to join the Chicago Climate Exchange, so we could "offset" greenhouse gas emissions. (My wife is adjusting the family menu to address my personal methane contribution.)

I'm exceptionally lazy, but cutting my greenhouse gas emissions nearly in half was easier than any boulder problem I've ever tried. And it's certainly worth the trouble if I can help preserve a place like the Rwenzoris, not to mention help tackle a few of our own environmental issues.

Counting Sheep

Doug Peacock

Editors' note: Doug Peacock is an author, Vietnam veteran, filmmaker, and naturalist who has written extensively on wilderness and wilderness issues, from grizzly bears to buffalo, from the Sierra Madre of the Sonoran Desert to the fjords of British Columbia, from the tigers of Siberia to the blue sheep of Nepal. Before becoming a writer, Doug was a Green Beret medic and the real-life model for Edward Abbey's George Washington Hayduke in The Monkey Wrench Gang. *His books include* Grizzly Years: In Search of the American Wilderness, In the Shadow of the Sabertooth, In the Presence of Grizzlies: The Ancient Bond Between Men and Bears, The Essential Grizzly: The Mingled Fates of Men and Bears, *and* Walking It Off: A Veteran's Chronicle of War and Wilderness. *Here, in "Counting Sheep," he discusses his encounters with elusive desert bighorn in southern Arizona over several decades.*

Insomnia has been the central dysfunction of my adult life and I go into the desert to sleep. I figure I have spent almost two years of my life sleeping under the stars among the cactus of the American southwest or on rare stormy nights in a tent off the desert coast of the Sea of Cortez. My favorite desert for sleeping, however, is the great expanse of country embracing the border of southwestern Arizona and Mexico, the uninhabited desert ranges and valleys of the Cabeza Prieta, one of the best places on earth to get a good night's sleep.

The Cabeza Prieta is just the name of a block of mountainous hills within an area of the same name now designated as a National Wildlife Refuge. This refuge is surrounded by identical looking wastelands managed by the National Park Service, the BLM, or used as a bombing range by the Marines and Air Force. It's all great country; the only road is Mexican Highway 2 just south of the border. I pay no attention whatsoever to these cultural, governmental, and otherwise artificial boundaries and have democratically thrown down my sleeping bag on about 220 different nights in washes on all sides of the fences.

The soporific device of counting sheep in order to fall asleep has never worked for me. Instead, I tend to log the constellations with a star chart or read by a tiny ironwood fire until drowsy. Some nights I just watch the celestial clock unfurl or think about a girl I used to know. Sheep never cross my mind until sometimes just at daybreak when the clatter of real desert bighorn sheep startles me fully awake.

This doesn't happen very often of course: four times, my notebooks say, four mountain sheep on four mornings spread over two decades. Desert bighorn aren't the kind of animal I see very often, although I run across their tracks nearly every time I visit the Cabeza Prieta. The sheep I see I invariably hear first. One of the best times to do this is in the morning from your sleeping bag though you can also hear them moving about on the scree and rocks towards evening.

The first desert bighorn I heard then saw from my sleeping bag was north of Buck Tank along a low spine of granitic hills running north into the bajada. It was daybreak on Christmas Day of 1979. I was still in the bag warming my fingers over the ironwood ashes of the previous night's fire. The sound of rock clattering on the ridge startled me. I reached for my field glasses and scanned the ridge for movement. The slope was bare with only a few creosote and *Bursera* trees dotting the hillside. I couldn't see anything. Suddenly I heard more racket and caught movement coming over the saddle. I saw what looked like a ghostly grey grizzly coming towards me. The animal's head had a curl of corrugated horn. The bear was a sheep, a ram with a full curl. I dropped the glasses and the bighorn caught the movement; the ram stopped and looked at me from twenty yards. As sunlight capped the tops of the highest peaks, the bighorn turned and ambled back across the crest of the ridge.

The reason I sleep well in the desert is probably because I walk so much out there. Travelling over the land on foot is absolutely the best way to see the country, scent its fragrance, feel its heat, and get to know its plants and animals; this simple activity is the great instructor of my life. I do my best thinking while walking—saving me countless thousands of dollars in occupational counseling, legal fees, and behavioral therapy—and the Cabeza Prieta is my favorite place in the world to walk.

I didn't always do so much walking out on the Cabeza Prieta. My first trips out there, beginning in the late sixties, were made in the usual fashion, driving a pickup across the Devil's Highway or easing a jeep up the sandy tracks of the spur roads.

Most of these trips and ninety percent of my several dozen non-solo visits to the Cabeza Prieta were taken with two close friends named Ed: Ed Gage and Ed Abbey. Later, when truck camping seemed tame and I needed a bit of adventure in my life, I decided to try to walk across the Cabeza Prieta alone, covering 120 to 165 miles, depending on the route I took. Taking it easy, I usually make the trip in about eleven days—ten nights free from insomnia, ten great nights of untroubled sleep.

In all, I've made seven of these trips, solo backpacking the area from Welton, Tacna, or the Tenaja Altas to Ajo, Organ Pipe, or Quitobaquito, sometimes vice versa, always by different routes, crossing all the big valleys, which, adding in the trips by vehicle, means I've spent over two hundred nights of my life sleeping out there.

On these desert treks, I average from about twelve to twenty miles per day. The mileage depends on the terrain, if I am fasting or low on food, and if I'm walking during daylight or by moonlight. Anything over twenty miles tends to rub raw spots into my aging body or bruise my feet, especially when I'm carrying my full load of water: three and one half gallons on the longer dry legs of the journey between the Sierra Pinta and Charlie Bell or Papago Well. My exact daily distance is whatever it takes to ensure the fatigue which banishes insomnia. Night walking is more exhausting because you need to brace yourself against injury; for instance, you have to lock your knee and ankle by tensing your quadriceps whenever you break through the honeycombed earth of rodent colonies under the creosote of the bajadas.

I keep crude journal notes of all this and tend to record such things as tracks and sightings of bighorn sheep—a very big deal to me. Actually, on my walks I saw few bighorn sheep but, as everyone knows, the best way to see sheep is to sit quietly, not walk with your nose at the level of the creosote. I did, however, see a lot of tracks.

What little I know of desert bighorn sheep has mostly been inferred from these tracks, although I've seen a few sheep too, counting almost three dozen bighorn sheep scattered throughout the desert ranges of the Cabeza Prieta during the past two decades. Ed Gage saw the first one just north of Cabeza Prieta tanks back in the winter of 1972, one of our first trips together. He had been sitting on a ridgetop reading Kazantzakis when he heard rock clattering on the slope above him. Gage looked up and saw a magnificent ram with a full curl amble down the ridge away from him, big scrotum swinging from side to side, he said, so he knew it was a ram as he had never seen a sheep before. The bighorn passed down the slope and disappeared below him.

My sheep count of thirty-four desert bighorns began in 1972 (I didn't see any the first three years) and ended in March of 1992.

Except for the ones I glimpsed from my sleeping bag, I saw all these sheep in precipitous terrain much like that of Gage's ram. My biggest count was a mixed herd of seven ewes and younger sheep one mile east of Half Way Tank in the Cabeza Prieta Mountains.

Once I saw four rams bedded together and facing out in the four directions on a spur ridge running off the Sierra Pinta into the Tule Desert north of Sunday Pass. I've seen pairs of desert bighorn three times—in the Growlers, the Agua Dulce, and Cabeza Prieta Mountains—and once a group of three ewes I startled near an outlier hill south of the Agila Mountains. The rest of the time my sightings have all been single animals.

The tracks are a different story. My field notes indicate sheep behavior I have never witnessed; sheep crossing the big valleys and using the creosote bajadas. I found repeated crossing of the Tule Desert by sheep using the same route during three different years: from the mouth of Smoke Tree Wash east to Isla Pinta. One of these crossing was made by a mixed herd of four or five ewes and two bighorn young. Other odd crossings include a ram from just south of Bean Pass trekking nonstop west along the Devil Hills to the north end of the Cabeza Prieta, a single sheep from the Agua Dulce by way of O'Neill Hills into the Pinta Sands, and two sets of bighorns tracks starting from an old, man-made pile of rocks, perhaps marking a very large grave, on the mid-eastern flank of the Granite Mountains across the Growler Valley and disappearing in the basaltic cobbles of the Growlers just north of Charlie Bell.

You would think bighorn sheep would be nervous out in these flats and open areas where they are vulnerable to predators. I've only seen circumstantial sign of sheep predation twice and both times it involved mountain lions. Lions are not common in this low desert where deer are not frequently found. The first time I saw the sign of a lion was on a trip with Ed Gage back in 1973 near one of the higher tanks of Tinajas Alta; this consisted only of a recent lion track near a much older disarticulated skeleton of a bighorn. The other, made while visiting Ed Abbey in 1990, was a dismembered carcass of a young sheep; there was indirect evidence the bighorn had been cached and lion scat and scrapings were found nearby.

The only times I've run into—actually I heard them—desert bighorn at night has been when the moon was big. Twice I was sitting quietly, and the other time I was backpacking by the light of the nearly full moon. I like to walk at night in the desert, especially when I'm having trouble sleeping. One such night, at the southern tip of the Copper Mountains, I heard the sound of clatter and rolling rocks, the dull clank of hooves coming from high on the slope. This racket had to be sheep moving on the hillside. What else could it be?

Sometimes I wonder how anybody ever manages to study desert sheep; I seem to have enough trouble just seeing them. When I'm up north, in Montana, British Columbia, or Alaska, I see bighorn sheep all the time. I see them in the spring down low in the valleys when snow still clogs the passes and slopes. Later, I watch them feeding and bedding on grassy ridges and avalanche chutes above timberline. Twice, I've found sheep carcasses buried by grizzlies and, though I have never seen a grizzly bear successfully chase and kill a bighorn, I once followed a big male grizzly in Glacier National Park who charged a herd of rams scattering them up the scree on up the cliffs behind Haystack Butte where the bear turned back. Even as late as November, I sometimes linger in grizzly country and watch the big rams clash, the clank of their hollow horns resounding into absorbent air of the snow-filled basins and gathering dusk of the Rocky Mountain Front near Many Glacier.

I've never seen any of that sort of thing in the desert. One March, from a great distance, I watched a three-quarter-curl ram south of Growler Peak probably browsing on lupine brush. At any rate, he was feeding, I couldn't be sure on what. During the spring of 1973, Ed Abbey and I found agave inflorescences in the Agua

Dulce chewed off by sheep and the remains of smashed barrel cactus near Sunday Pass with sheep tracks all around. But what desert bighorn eat from day to day has always been a mystery to me.

All this sheep lore doesn't add up to much spread over thirty years. To me, the sudden appearance of desert bighorn sheep has always been a mystery, a blessing, sometimes a specter bearing just the edge of fear. Despite my cryptic field notes, my memory of sheep in the past twenty years is shriveled to those who roused me from my sleeping bag and startled me on the brilliant nights of the full moon. Those sheep, it seems, I had to earn.

Even sheep sign can be a gift. Twenty years ago Ed Gage and I found a sheep track outside a mine shaft southeast of Papago Well. Inside the fifty-year-old hole was an old case of dynamite, the nitroglycerin all sweated out and dangerously unstable. Nearby, at Bassarisc Tank, we found more sheep tracks and the paw print of a lion; suddenly, the entire desert was imbued with unseen power and danger.

During December of 1974, Ed Abbey and I drove my pickup into the Cabeza Prieta. Ed and I were unattached and without families at the time. We had spent a sniffling, lonely Christmas Eve at a topless bar in Tucson drinking whiskey. Thinking we could improve on that, we packed up and drove 150 miles west over Charlie Bell Pass into the Cabeza Prieta. We sipped beer all the way from Three Forks and were a tad plastered by the time we hit Charlie Bell Pass. We got my 1966 Ford truck stuck several times creeping down the dark treacherous road to the well, hanging up the ass end of the truck, jacking it up in the dark, rocking it free, and then dropping down into the Growler Valley. We continued on for one more six-pack around the north end of the Granite Mountains where we got stuck in the sand one last time, finally crawling into our sleeping bags shortly after midnight. At six in the morning, a sheriff's search-and-rescue team roared up looking for some high school kids some criminal son-of-a-bitch had hired to collect 20- and 40-mm brass military cartridges. When a helicopter flew over, this bastard had driven off, ditching the kids. One of kids, we later learned, died of thirst and exposure. The search team pulled us out of the sand and went on. Ed and I drove through Montrose Well west into the Mohawk Valley. At the low pass we found bighorn sheep tracks. Later, on New Year's Eve at Eagle Tank, it sleeted and snowed on us—an unusual occurrence. We stayed three days in the Sierra Pinta, then dropped south into the Pinecate lava fields, a place of black basalt.

Years later, I followed the tracks of a desert sheep from the bottom of Temporal Pass in the Growler Mountains to the center of the Growler Wash where I lost the trail. I had gotten out there by walking southwest from Ajo after I had taken the bus from Tucson. I had come on a one-way ticket purchased for me by Lisa, the woman I later married. The Greyhound Bus clerk had been reluctant to even sell her the ticket for me.

"Lady," the clerk had said to Lisa, "nobody buys a one-way ticket to Ajo."

At Ajo I shouldered my backpack and disappeared over the mine tailings, passing the camp of the O'odham hermit, Chico Shunie, just before daylight. It was dark again the next night when I reached the bottom of the Growler Valley. Even by the dim light of the moon I could see big pieces of Hohokam pottery and *Glycymeris* clam shells lying on the desert pavement—the "Lost City" of the Hohokam shell-trekkers. From here in the Growler Valley, an ancient shell trail ran south to Bahia Adair on the Sea of Cortez and north to the Gila River near Picture Rocks where the most common animal petroglyph motif was that of desert sheep. I lost the trail of the bighorn because of the darkness and because a rattlesnake nailed me in the calf that night, though the snake-bite turned out to be a dry one. The next day, with a story to tell, I walked out twenty miles to Papago Well where Clarke and Ed Abbey were waiting for me.

Shortly after Gage's death, the man—a mutual friend—who co-founded the Sanctuary Movement asked me to consider "taking over the Southwest Sector." This meant illegally leading small groups of refugees, mostly from El Salvador, from Highway 2 in Mexico north through the Cabeza Prieta up towards Interstate 8 or to some other point where they could be picked up by vehicle. I agonized long and hard over this decision. I had already begun my work with grizzly bears and I knew enough about myself from radical politics in the sixties and later in Vietnam to figure out where my talents didn't lie and the exhausting dangers of over-committing myself. Still, this was something I could do and it needed doing.

The dilemma tore at me and I couldn't sleep. Once again, I went into the Cabeza Prieta to slumber and to track the sign that would show me what to do. The bus dropped me off on the Tacna off-ramp. I shouldered my backpack draped with three gallon canteens and staggered into the creosote headed towards Mexico. I skirted the Copper Mountains, passed Buck Mountain, and, at the mouth of A-1 Wash, I found the corrugated remains of a giant set of ram's horns. The next morning I followed another sheep's tracks south up the wash until I passed over the tiny divide into the inner valley north of the tanks where Gage had seen his ram.

Sooner or later everyone runs into death and I ran into a lot of it early on. And so I have used this great desert to bargain with the departed and get a handle on my insomnia. It's true, I invent ceremonies when necessary, especially when my own culture provides none; I erect my own memorials and celebrate my own Day of the Dead. But mostly, I just shoulder a backpack and walk beyond fatigue across the bajadas, maybe crossing a set of sheep tracks and following them up a wash, finding a perfect campsite. The story of this place is not of loss but renewal.

The Cabeza Prieta desert is the most important thing Ed Abbey, Ed Gage, and I ever shared and it is no coincidence that these two closest desert friends from the past two decades are out there. Gage was a tough one because he was a suicide; I maintain a secret and no doubt illegal memorial for Gage on a hilltop in one of these desert valleys. Each year for seven years I took a hike to visit this monument and hold a private ceremony.

The last time Ed Abbey smiled was when I told him where he was going to be buried, and I smile too when I think of this small favor, this last simple task friends can do for one another—the rudimentary shovel work, this sweaty labor consummating trust, finally testing the exact confirmation by lying down in the freshly dug grave to check out the view, bronze patina of boulder behind limb of palo verde and turquoise sky beyond branch of torote, then receiving a sign: seven buzzards soaring above joined by three others, all ten banking over the volcanic rubble and riding the thermal up the flank of the mountain, gliding out and over the distant valley. Even three years later, I grin as I crest the ridge above his grave, the earth falls away and mountain ranges stretch off into the grey distance as far as the eye can see; there is not a human sign or sound, only a faint desert breeze stirring the blossoms of brittlebush. We should be so lucky.

On the eve of March 16th, I journeyed to the edge of this desert place. March 16th is a "Day of the Dead" for me, the anniversary of the My Lai massacre (I was twenty miles away in Vietnam that day) and also the day in 1989 three friends and myself buried Ed Abbey here, illegally, in accordance with his last wishes.

I had travelled out here alone to Ed's grave, bearing little gifts, including a bottle of mescal and a bowl of pozole verde I had made myself. I sat quietly on the black volcanic rocks listening to the desert silence, pouring mescal over the grave and down my throat until the moon came up an hour or so before midnight. Suddenly I heard a commotion to the south, the roar of basaltic scree thundering down the slope opposite me. A large solitary animal was headed my way.

I got the hell out of there.

Two days later I told my story of the desert bighorn ram I heard but never saw to my poet friend Jim Harrison.

"Well, Doug," Jim said, "maybe it was old Ed."

Backing Into My Inner Om

Peter McBride

Editors' note: A Colorado native, Pete McBride has spent almost two decades studying the world with his camera. A self-taught, award-winning photographer, writer, and filmmaker, he has traveled on assignment to over sixty countries for the publications of the National Geographic Society, Smithsonian, Outside, Men's Journal, Esquire, Stern, *and many others. Currently he is a contributing editor for* National Geographic Traveler. *McBride is best known for documenting his local river, the Colorado. His journey culminated in an acclaimed coffee table book:* The Colorado River: Flowing Through Conflict; *an award-winning short film,* Chasing Water; *and scores of essays about water scarcity. When not lost on assignment, you can find Pete exploring the creeks and mountains around Colorado. Due to his experiences in India writing "Backing Into My Inner Om," he continues to practice yoga and now owns a Royal Enfield motorcycle.*

High above the silvery flow of the Ganges River, on a creaky suspension bridge in the Himalaya, I realize how far I have strayed from my quest. The metronome sound of a Royal Enfield motorcycle ticking beneath my legs is the giveaway. I'd come to the remote hamlet of Rishikesh, India—the gateway to the Himalaya—with a vision of deep silence and lots of focused, healing yoga. Yet something, kharmic power perhaps, lured me slightly astray.

Straddling the Ganges River at the base of the foothills, Rishikesh is a shopping mall of spirituality. For those seeking enlightenment or just adventurous escape—be it hippies, spiritual tourists, river rats, or religious pilgrims—the healing power of the Ganges attracts hundreds of thousands each year. As a result, Rishikesh and its neighboring big brother, Haridwar, are pulsing hotspots brimming with ashrams, yoga schools, whitewater rafting companies, and vegan restaurants. By law, the region is vegetarian and alcohol free. In 1968, the Beatles came here to study transcendental meditation. Ringo Starr left early, but John, Paul, and George stayed for weeks at Maharishi Yogi's ashram and wrote some four dozen songs. Many found their way onto the White Album.

I didn't come to write music but to retune an ailing back. Years of contact sports and the immutable milestones of aging appeared a couple years ago in the shape of a persistent, jarring pain in my lower spine. After I'd endured the cracks of chiropractors, the pricks of acupuncturists, even the tearful kneading of Rolfers, an X-ray finally revealed what looked to be a photo of Jenga—that wooden block tower game—except my vertebrae were the blocks. One vertebrae stuck disturbingly inward more than the rest. According to the doctor, the condition is somewhat common. But if I didn't stabilize the area with core strength and stretching, I would be forced to fuse my lower spine—metal rods, surgery. Not plan A . . . or B.

Yoga, I was told, might help. Having grown up on a cattle ranch in central Colorado, I forged some less-than-limber muscles by loading hay bales and competing in sports like ice hockey, ski racing, and mountain biking. My idea of stretching involved a few toe touches—okay, shin touches maybe. Sure, I attended my handful of power yoga, vinyasa flow, even Bikram classes where the room temperature exceeds 100 degrees Fahrenheit. The American yoga scene offers a good workout, but, frankly, it was too distracting. Having been that sweaty guy in the back of the studio, struggling to keep up and often more focused on the shapely figures in front of me than my breath, the therapeutic value was limited.

Rishikesh, "the capital of yoga," and the purifying Ganges water, I decided, could be my remedy. I would put my beef-eating, coffee- and wine-guzzling habits on hold and embrace the ashram/yogi lifestyle in its motherland. Prepared to contort body and mind, I set off to find my inner Om. What did I have to lose? Back surgery, for starters.

The distracting rumble of a motorcycle, of course, was not part of the yoga retune. The magnetic powers of a classic British bike (built in India) didn't necessarily pull me off my plan; its temptations just lured me on a path slightly counter to my quest.

Motoring in second gear, I glide through dense traffic on the swaying suspension bridge. Foot commuters—some barefoot, others ornate with painted sandals and jeweled toes beneath swishing wraps—whisper as I weave past and around the wheeled and hoofed traffic—mopeds and sacred cows clattering across loose, weathered planks. There is such spatial awareness that oncoming handlebars (even horns) occasionally chime yet avoid entanglement. Rhesus monkeys, hanging from steel cables above, study every move of every passerby, looking to snatch food, jewels, or any shiny object.

Leaving the bridge, I rumble down the alley and turn into the back courtyard of Parmarth Niketan Ashram.

I've been in residence here for three days and am in the groove—feeling smack center in the present moment. I'd chosen Parmarth because it is less strict than other ashrams allowing you to come and go as you like. Just be back before curfew. I was also impressed by its mission to offer free medical care to those in dire need. Parmarth also supports 200 orphaned/impoverished boys called Rishikumaras, providing housing, food, and Vedic teachings.

At 6:50 a.m. the next morning I sit Indian style, in a simple room with a wooden floor, white walls, a metal ceiling, and poster-size black-and-white photos of Swami Chidanand Saraswati smiling down on our small group of students. Swamiji, as he is known, left home at age eight to study in the Himalaya. A winner of the Mahatma Gandhi Humanitarian award, he now is the spiritual head of Parmarth. He doesn't teach classes but is occasionally on the scene in the evening. (I would have the honor of making his acquaintance twice during my stay.) As I listen to my yoga teacher, an American, I quietly work on my Hatha pranayama, a breathing technique that involves inhaling and exhaling through one nostril at a time.

Patience. Breathe.

As I move into "mountain" pose (downward dog in the U.S.), I focus on absences. There are no New Age tunes pumping through hidden speaker, no distracting yoga outfits, no blinding heat, no incense, and no attitude. Just students and a teacher. Before I came, I knew something about the cultural divide between American and Indian yoga. With the Yankee infatuation with fitness, some say American yoga stretches more in the direction of exercise. Others argue it is all part of yoga's ongoing evolution. Whatever, I tackle the asanas wearing a down jacket and long pants. Throughout much of the year, Rishikesh is hot, at times scorching. But it is December, with frigid mornings. My neighbors, fixated on their breath, are equally bundled, some even swaddled in blankets. For some it is their first yoga class ever. I know I am only competing against my own body, but I am relieved to know I am not the lone rookie. Initially I miss the music but quickly become aware of the Himalayan rhythms around us: glacial gusts clanking the studio's wooden shutters and the scurrying of monkeys playing on the metal roof.

After class, I meet Ramya, one of two American yoga teachers at the ashram. She came here on a sabbatical after her children left the nest. I ask her about yoga's cultural divide. She smiles and offers, "There is a saying: Yoga came to change America, but America changed yoga." As I digest the comment, I embrace my first off-the mat yogi test—eating. With little choice, my appetite submits to the Vedic diet of alkaline foods: lentils, rice, cooked veggies, spices. I also quickly grow fond the code of silence during mealtime. It is broken only by the symphony of utensils on aluminum plates and the recorded mantra chants played on a 9-volt radio next to the serving line.

The coffee withdrawal, at first, is cruel. The other staggering hurdle is eating cross-legged on a marble floor. My hips detest it. Small tables, maybe eight inches high, are a luxury offered mostly for Westerners. They provide little comfort for my screaming hips and back. During one meal, a regular ashram visitor from Brazil named Abrau points out how horridly fast I eat.

"I used to eat like you; fast as I could to get to something else."

"I know, my tapeworm is quite active," I say smiling. He doesn't laugh. "Kidding, bad habit. Actually, I am trying to finish my meal before my hip or knee dislocates from contorting to fit to this marble floor."

He laughs. "Si, just remember, your digestion is not in a hurry."

"Noted. Thanks." I felt an urge to remind Abrau about that code of silence at mealtime.

Patience. Breathe.

Over the next few days, I drift through a pattern of waking to the ashram's meditative mantra chants starting at 5 a.m. (heard mostly from bed), attending cold yoga classes before breakfast, and eating meals in silence (slightly slower). I also begin leaving the sprawling ashram on exploratory sorties around Rishikesh and neighboring Haridwar.

It is beyond the ashram walls where I discovered my secret meditation weapon—the Royal Enfield motorcycle. I'd found its source, Madhav, earlier via Facebook. Raised in an ashram himself, Madhav abandoned the austere path the day he arrived in Rishikesh. He claims that "the power of the Ganges was so high, I couldn't depart." Today, he does the logistical heavy lifting for large groups visiting the area. He also helps with random requests from visitors like me. After repeatedly asking him the best way to get from A to B, he finally asked, gently, "Peter, would a motorcycle work for you?" When I meet Madhav, he is smiling next to my British-designed-Indian-built 500cc motorcycle, a shimmering classic. I can't decide which looks nicer, my motorized magic carpet ride or my new friend, the clean shaven, big smiling Madhav. I offer to pay for the rental in advance. Madhav smiles gently, gives a slight head wobble, and responds, "No problem, Peter. You pay later." Immediately, I realized Madhav is one of those local gems you never want to lose, even after you have returned home.

On my first outing, I explore the crumbling ashram where the Beatles lived. As I wander the ruins, I wonder where Lennon wrote "Dear Prudence." The lyrics ("won't you come out to play") are said to be a plea to friend Prudence Farrow, Mia's sister, to snap out of a recluse state of meditation. I use Lennon's words to validate my motorcycle venture.

During sunsets, I glide down narrow, bustling streets or enjoy the singing at aarti—the Hindi "happy hour"—a daily ceremony on the banks of the Ganges. Scores of Indians peppered with curious travelers sing Hindi hymns and swirl ornate lanterns to seal prayers before splashing Ganges water on their feet. Some offer their prayers via candles that float downstream in miniature boats made of leaves as a looming white statue of Shiva, the all powerful Hindi yogi deity, looks on.

Despite such blissful days, I anxiously wonder if the yoga classes would get more challenging. Would I learn some spine-curing contortions and become more limber? Not once had I even broken a sweat in class, despite my down jacket. Was I missing something? My back ached.

Patience. Breathe.

After yoga class one morning, I bump into Madhav. He continues to help me navigate the area, steering me to the best cup of maisala chai or the freshest, belly-safe salad (Romana's Garden). I express my concerns about my therapy.

"Peter, remember, yoga is more about the mind than the body." He pauses. "And don't worry so much," he says with an easy, toothy grin, his perfectly shaved head almost glowing as he smiles. "Remember, worry is praying for what you don't want."

After a week on the ashram routine, I leave camp and motor up the Ganges.

Stay left, stay left, stay left quickly becomes my mantra as I wind past candy-striped buses and overstuffed rickshaws belching black clouds. Madhav had said that the Ganges' power strengthens farther upstream, where cave dwellings are not unusual. Winding north, I focus on the Enfield's rattling vibrations as I pass bands of rhesus monkeys fearlessly sitting in the road, awaiting scraps. I avoid rock falls and lean into hairpin corners, nearly scraping my toes. In sections the road shadows the Ganges; in others the green glacial waters are hundreds of feet below churning beneath over-hung cliffs. I grin constantly.

Breathe. Relax. Stay left.

Cars and trucks pass three abreast shrilling trumpet-like horns that echo off the mountains. Despite many reckless passes and near misses, the flow of chaotic karma moves up this most dangerous road in the Himalaya. Road signs with cursive letters offer yogi-like reminders of safety: "License to drive, not to fly."

As the sun stretches into an orange ball on the horizon, I arrive at the entrance to the Vashista cave. Thought to be the oldest meditative cave in the region, some call it the birthplace of conscious thought.

As the sun drops, I notice a sinewy man cloaked in the saffron robes of a sadhu. I approach and ask if he can help. He opens his arms warmly and says, "I'm sadhu, leave bike with me." In my mind, a red flag shoots skyward. While saffron robes generally signify "holy man" or one who has renounced the material world, many rumors circulate that criminals use these same robes as cover when in hiding. Flash decision time—I stay with Madhav's non-worry approach.

"Okay, I'll be back in a few days, and I'll tip you nicely. Keep an eye on my baby." With that, my new Enfield keeper smiles. I walk to the river and up the stone beach to find the rowboat ferry to shuttle me across the Ganges, where I will spend two days at a small retreat.

Anand Lok is a seven-room guest lodge cantilevered over the Ganges, roughly 200 feet above its swirling waters. It sits on the edge of Cirasu, a village with no roads, no vehicles, and only one pedestrian jula (bridge) connecting it to the modern world.

The most intoxicating smile I've witnessed greets me on arrival. Jigdish, the manager, is excited to have a few guests during off-season.

For the next two days, two fellow Parmarth visitors—one Dutch, one Chilean—and I walk along the Ganges, drink pots of chai to ward off the evening/early-morning chill, and play with schoolchildren in the village. Throughout India, the poverty can be alarming, overwhelming even. Its bony hand permeates every corner, and it doesn't ignore the village of Ciralu. However, the smiling face of Jigdish and his neighbors offer testimony to the wealth of contentment in their world of little. Like many sustainable villages, they are poor in dollars yet rich in spirit and appear remarkably happy.

I ask Jigdish if he does yoga.

"Yes, every day, work is my yoga, running this hotel keeps my body flowing."

Motivated to keep my yoga flowing, I do sun salutations on a sandy Ganges beach one morning. A village teenager, who speaks little English, decides to drop his firewood chores and join me. As if on cue, this rippling, muscled teen closes his eyes and falls backwards, folding into an arching backbend. "Wow," I mutter.

Unable to communicate through our language rift, we speak via yoga poses and laughter. After a while, I point to the river and say "swim?" The boy answers with a head wobble—that ubiquitous Indian gesture, which I grow to loosely understand as "very good."

Under clear, crisp blue skies we strip down to just boxers and dash into the icy waters of the Ganges. The blast of cold immediately steals my air and pierces me awake. Swimming in the Ganges is believed to be purifying—not just physically but symbolically, washing away any prior sins. My new swimming companion and I let out whoops as we clamor back to shore. I can't say if my sins vanish, but I feel electrified.

"Heeeello?" I say hesitantly as I enter total darkness. Rookie move. Clearly not the best way to enter an ancient meditation cave. No one answers.

I'd left my swimming pal, Jigdish, his guests, and the smiling world of village life to recross the Ganges and spend time inside the Vashista Cave, which is said to go beyond history into mythology. Shuffling through the cool, sweet air, across grain sack flooring, I stop near candlelight. I sit down, cross-legged, and try to relax and breathe. With eyes closed, I focus on just my breathing for the first time in my life. My mind quickly strays. Why am I here? Has the sadhu stolen my bike?

Relax. Just a rental. Breathe.

I return focus to my lungs. A mental rhythm aligns with my breath. I open my eyes. Suddenly, I see the entire cave. I am alone at the end of long tunnel-like passageway. Tokens of worship sit near candles on a stone altar. The air tastes even sweeter, fresher now.

Outside, I glance at the time. My mental clock guesstimates I have meditated for roughly 10 minutes. It has been over 50. Where did I go?

The cave's caretaker sits in the sun. A sacred cow lingers nearby. I feel hyperaware. I thank the caretaker and he mentions how lucky I am to be alone. The cave frequently attracts tour groups of 50, sometimes 100, visitors a day.

Parked just as I had left her, the shiny Enfield sits up the hill, unharmed, off the trail. As I walk up, my bike keeper magically appears.

"See, no problem. Bike here. I'm sadhu. Money."

I happily hand over a wad of rupees—about $5 U.S. He shuffles his saffron robe, quickly burying the notes in a fold, then says, "More. Hungry." I peel a few more notes, which he gingerly takes before disappearing toward the river. I tally the parking cost: $7.

On first kick, my mythological bike rumbles to life. Feeling almost drugged from my Vashista time warp, I float back down the Himalayan highway, meditating on the road.

Stay left. Stay left. Stay left.

Riding now by instinct, feeling what I can't help but call "biker Zen," I swerve past cows, their calves, street vendors, scooters, sadhus, hippies, and healers. I keep meditating on my antique cruiser and the planks ahead, maintaining a laser awareness about my surroundings and my existence at that exact time in space. I've missed my friend Madhav and the ashram.

But before I return, I take one more quick side trip.

Hidden in the hills just west of Rishikesh, the Ananda Spa has gained the reputation as the "best spa in the world." Originally a palace of the Maharaja of Tehri Garhwal, it is now a five-star hotel. Curious, I rumble up the mountainside.

The road to Ananda Spa warrants its own title: "Most Enlightened Road Signs." One sign reads, "Road Is Hilly, Don't Be Silly." Another, "After Whiskey, Driving Risky." I feel like I have the Dali Lama whispering in my ear as I rumble up the mountain.

The whiskey reference is odd in light of the dry county regulations, but I later learn that Ananda Spa sits above the county line, thus booze is available. Can I sustain my new yogi discipline?

When I roll into the ornate reception entrance dazzled with manicured flowers, past a security gate, a helicopter pad, and a kilted Indian soldier playing bagpipes (a throwback to Colonial times), I garner a few looks.

"Does the valet take motorcycles?" I ask, casually.

"Of course. We love Enfields," the manager answers. He adds, "But I must say, you are the first to arrive by bike. Very unique."

I spend only a day at the Ananda Spa, and must say, every bit of it is luxuriously five-star. I eat decadent Indian cuisine (staying true to my new diet), learn about ayurvedic dosha (yoga's cousin), and experience one ayurvedic treatment. Two men karate chopped my back with herb-filled bags dipped in hot oils. The only herb that had an English translation—cumin. It made my back sore, but looser.

Somewhat reluctant to leave the five-star bubble, I motor down the hill to the chaotic vitality that defines India.

I arrive at the start of the evening aarti. Led by some of his coworkers and the young Rishikumaras who live here, Swamiji walks by.

"You're back, Peter."

Slightly surprised, I mutter, "Yes. Nice to see you again, Swami."

With long, flowing salt-and-pepper hair and beard to accompany, he glides past me, his saffron robes swaying. His physical frame is small, yet his presence towers.

"Welcome home," he adds, glowing. I return my best head wobble.

Later that night I find Madhav. He is helping organize logistics for a large international party. The schedule is tight and Madhav was hired to make sure everything clicks like clockwork—not easy in the Indian time zone. As I wait to catch up, he is hounded with requests.

Madhav answers each with grace and a friendly "can do" yogi cool.

In the famous 700-verse Hindi scripture, the Bhagavad-Gita, Prince Arjuna profoundly discusses life and duty with his chariot driver before heading into battle. Toward the end, the chariot driver reveals himself to be Lord Krishna, the Supreme Being. As I watch Madhav, it occurs to me that this quiet, ever-smiling man standing in front me—my new friend who has effortlessly guided me throughout my entire trip—is my symbolic chariot driver (alright, motorcycle renter, travel advisor), helping unearth my inner Om.

Sure, many of the lessons I experienced—stretch, breathe, eat slower/healthier (less coffee even), and relax—are simple. And, yes, replacing the stresses of too much work and too much TV/computer screen time with crisp swims in sacred, glacial waters followed by time-warps in caves and motorcycle glides through Himalayan foothills could give most folks a greater peace of mind (unless, of course, you fear motorcycles).

Yet Madhav was the walking example of that gentle soul I aspired to be. Nothing, no matter the urgency or size, derailed him. He didn't live in a cave nor did he guide me through a single pretzel contortion or simple "mountain" pose. Yet I realize he taught me, almost daily, not necessarily how to walk the "yogi path" but to understand it better and most important, that my mind needs as much stretching as my annoying back.

After two weeks of daily yoga, I can now touch my toes and even sit cross-legged through a meal. My back? The persistent, unfriendly pain did not entirely vanish. But it has notably subsided. Did my spine actually start to heal? I don't know, but neither I nor my inner Om worry about it.

Monte Sarmiento

Stephen Venables

Editors' note: Stephen Venables is best known for his part in the 1988 Anglo-American-Canadian expedition that made a spectacular new route up Mount Everest's biggest wall, the Kangshung Face. There were only four climbers on the team, and Stephen was the only one to make it all the way to the summit, without supplementary oxygen. However, some of his most rewarding expeditions have been to little-known peaks in remote valleys. His Himalayan first ascents include Kishtwar Shivling, Panch Chuli V, Solu Tower, Chorten Peak, and Ngabong Terong—the last two climbed solo—as well as new routes on Pungpa Ri and Kusum Kanguru. He has also climbed extensively in the European Alps, Africa, and South America. In recent years Venables has co-led several yacht-based expeditions to Antarctica and South Georgia with the internationally renowned yachtsman Skip Novak. During an earlier visit to the island, he took part in the giant-screen movie Shackleton's Antarctic Adventure *with Conrad Anker and Reinhold Messner. He also wrote the screenplay for the giant-screen movie* The Alps *and has appeared in television documentaries for BBC, ITV, and National Geographic. Venables is a former president of the world's oldest mountaineering institution, The Alpine Club. He has published twelve books, the first of which,* Painted Mountains, *won the prestigious Boardman Tasker Prize. More recently both* Himalaya Alpine Style *and his autobiography,* Higher Than the Eagle Soars, *won prizes at the Banff Mountain Film and Book Festival.*

Tierra del Fuego was a crazy idea. I love climbing but these days I rarely have the chance to get away. For my first expedition in three years I should have chosen somewhere warm, dry and accessible—a place to maximise the climbing potential of each precious day. Instead, I chose perversely to visit a remote, sodden, wind-battered island at the southern tip to Patagonia, knowing that in one month I would be lucky to get two or three days of actual climbing. Why on earth did I do it?

The answer, of course, is that there is more to climbing expeditions than the individual pitches of rock and ice. A mountain is often just an excuse to visit an interesting place and, after years of Alpine and Himalayan ventures, I find myself drawn increasingly to the Southern Hemisphere, in particular the wild mountains on the fringes of Antarctica. In 1990 I spent three months on the island of South Georgia, relishing the combination of mountain, sea and teeming wildlife, and learning to live with the almost incessant wind. Tierra del Fuego would be similar but with the added attraction of trees, for although it is glaciated country on the same latitude as South Georgia, the toe of South America is dipped in slightly warmer water. Those few extra degrees of warmth—and the infinite humidity of the Pacific weather system—nurture a glorious profusion of temperate rainforest which cloaks the intricate shoreline of the world's most extensive system of coastal channels.

So I was drawn by the landscape. More importantly, I was attracted to the team, which originated serendipitously, many thousands of miles away, on Everest. In 1988 I spent three of the happiest months of my life climbing a new route on the Kangshung Face with an American team. Five years later two of my companions were back on the mountain, this time on the north side, camped alongside John Roskelley and Jim Wickwire, telling them all the old yarns about their days on the Kangshung with an oddball Brit called Venables. Soon after that a letter arrived in England from

Wickwire, asking whether I would be interested in joining him and Roskelley on a trip to Monte Sarmiento, in Tierra del Fuego.

With our introverted psyche, it is a truism for Britons to talk about American "openness" and "friendliness"; but on my first American expedition there really had been a refreshing warmth and generosity of spirit, which I remembered fondly. Wickwire's letter promised more of the same and when I eventually met him in England I knew that a trip with him would be fun. I was not quite so sure about Roskelley, the self-confessed redneck from Spokane, whom I had not yet met, but who carried a reputation for seeing life in simple absolutes. This was a man who had frequently upset the American climbing establishment with his outspoken criticisms, a man who seemed, by all accounts, intolerant of fools and weaklings. How would he take to an oversensitive, unfit Englishman, only just recovering from a bad knee injury, sustained in a Himalayan accident? How would I match up to one of the world's toughest and most successful mountaineers?

I was curious, intrigued and a little apprehensive when I left home at the beginning of April, forsaking the English spring for fall in Patagonia. Arriving in Punta Arenas two days later, my apprehension evaporated immediately. Roskelley was open, friendly, uncomplicated, funnily observant with a quiet, dry Clint Eastwood voice. The eyes twinkled flirtatiously at Chilean waitresses, but it was the harmless joking of a man who is actually fiercely loyal to his wife and who spends the greater part of his life at home on the farm, looking after his two children. There was a lot of talk of home, both from him and Wickwire, who for thirty years has sustained a brilliant juggling act, balancing the demands of a large family in Seattle, an ambitious climbing career and a successful law practice representing Indian and Eskimo land rights in Alaska.

The fourth climber arriving in Punt Arenas was Tim Macartney-Snape, who led the first Australian ascent of Everest in 1984. He is a backwoods natural—tall, lean, self-contained, with huge lungs and an unerring competence lurking beneath an apparently diffident manner. An outstanding mountaineer, he is also experienced with boats and when we arrived at Ushuaia on the Beagle Channel he quickly endeared himself to the fifth team member, Charlie Porter, whose yacht, *Gondwana*, Wickwire had chartered for the expedition.

Twenty years ago Charlie Porter was a big name—a very big name—in Yosemite, where he spent countless days, often alone, hammering, hooking, drilling and jiggery-pokering his way up what were then some of the hardest artificial big wall climbs on El Capitan. Two of his routes in particular, The Shield and Zodiac, have become famous classics. His 1977 swansong was a phenomenal solo effort on Mt Asgard, in Baffin Island. Then he vanished from the climbing world, and headed south to Chile, where he embarked on a nine-month, two-thousand-mile solo kayak trip through the Patagonian channels. He has been in Chile ever since, kayaking, sailing, botanising, geologising, occasionally climbing and generally immersing himself in one of the world's most beautiful wildernesses. In these days of increasingly off-the-shelf adventure, he remains a true original—eccentric, opinionated and infectiously enthusiastic about the land that he has made his home.

This was our guide and skipper for the "scenic tour" up the Beagle Channel—that improbable creek which links Atlantic and Pacific, winding between Tierra del Fuego's main Isla Grande and a maze of smaller islands to the south and west. For five days we motored into the wind, occasionally hoisting the jib when the direction changed. In memory the days blur into a slow moving picture of black water, blue ice and reddening leaves of *Nothofagus pumilla*—one of the southern beech species—intermingled with dark evergreen *Nothofagus betuloides*. Each evening we would anchor in a cove, landlubbers fumbling with ropes, as Charlie shouted orders. Only Tim was really trusted; Roskelley and

Wickwire dared not so much as touch a rope and slouched around like disgraced schoolboys, calling themselves "The Stooges."

On the fourth day we battered through the grey lumpy water of the Bahia Desolada. Then on the final day we rounded the Brecknock Peninsula and emerged briefly on the Pacific coast of Chile, to feel the oceanic surge of waves that come all the way from Australia, before slinking back east into the shelter of the Cockburn Channel for the final run into Sarmiento.

The main group of peaks on Tierra del Fuego is named after the naturalist who came here in the *Beagle* in 1832 at the start of a voyage which would result eventually in a book challenging the whole basis of Western civilisation. Just west of the Cordillera Darwin, isolated on its own little peninsula, rises another peak, Monte Sarmiento, which is perhaps the most spectacular in Tierra del Fuego. It is certainly the most prominent and was described in Darwin's *The Voyage of the Beagle* as "the most conspicuous and the most splendid object in these regions. Rising abruptly from the sea to a height of about 7,000 feet it terminates in two sharp peaks, which seem absolutely in the sky, so lofty does the mountain appear when you are close to its base."

Those twin peaks of Sarmiento have eluded many expeditions over the last 126 years, since Domingo Lovisato first explored the south-west approaches in 1869. The first climbing attempt was led by Martin Conway in 1898, but he never really got to grips with— nor even saw—the upper slopes of the mountain.

Conway was followed by a man whose name is synonymous with Patagonia—Alberto de Agostini. Agostini spent the best part of his life away from his native Italy, serving in Patagonia as a Salesian missionary. An assiduous photographer, he posed stilted groupings of the native Indians, scrubbed clean and decked out in unnaturally fine furs; but his mountain photographs make no attempt to tame the grandeur of the wild landscape. For over forty years he explored the length and breadth of Patagonia, mapping, photographing and climbing. Of all his first ascents, the most important was probably the magnificent peak of San Lorenzo, between the two Patagonian icecaps. Down in Tierra del Fuego he led expeditions to several peaks including Sarmiento. The first Sarmiento attempt was in 1913 and the second in 1956, when he was seventy-three. On that second attempt Clemente Maffei and Carlo Mauri attained the South Ridge and finally succeeded on a very steep, direct line up spectacular rime mushrooms to the higher East Peak (2235m). The West Peak eluded three further Italian expeditions until a fourth, in 1986, was successful; Daniele Bosisio, Marco Della Santa, Mario Panzeri and Paolo Vitali reached the summit by its North-West Ridge. A British attempt on the East Peak in 1993, led by Caradoc Jones, was unsuccessful.

That was the state of play when we now arrived in April 1995. Each night in the cabin of *Gondwana*, Charlie had squinted through his stereoscope at aerial photos, convincing us that the original south-western approach up the Lovisato valley was our best bet; so we anchored in the nearest cove to the mouth of the Lovisato River, Stooges looking on while Charlie trussed up his precious *Gondwana* in a spider's web of shore lines, tied off to every tree in sight. Finally he chuckled happily, "If she moves now, she'll take the whole forest with her. What d'ya think Tim, huh?"

Macartney-Snape nodded his approval and we all went ashore, leaving the boat in charge of Minos, the French-Cretan cook. So far we had seen no sign of our mountain, nor indeed any high mountains. Dank, grey drizzle was to remain the pattern for most of our trip and when the mountain did finally appear, it was only in brief, flirtatious glimpses. From a climbing point of view it was frustrating; the only way to cope was to immerse oneself (literally) in the experience and learn to love the soft light, the dripping trees, the oozing emerald and orange bog, the glisten of jade green lichen, festooned luxuriantly in the forest where we made our home, a few yards from the beach. Charlie introduced us to the peppery taste of Canello leaves—"full of vitamin C, the Indians ate lots of 'em"—and the bittersweet Calafate berries. Macartney-Snape wielded the axe, building our kitchen and the bridge over the River Lovisato—two wildly-flexing *Nothofagus* trunks, lashed a few inches above the vicious glacial torrent.

Roskelley, mindful of the French mountaineer Poincenot, drowned near Fitzroy, wasn't too sure about the bridge at first. "I don't want anyone taking risks: it's not worth dying just to have a mountain named after yourself." Eventually he agreed that we should use the bridge, provided that no-one ever crossed it alone. All the while Wickwire, expedition leader, remained low profile. One night, sitting round the fire at base camp with wet cagoules and gumboots steaming on the line, I asked him why he didn't get a grip and tell us all what to do. He looked up from his book of poetry and said, "I wouldn't dream of telling you lot what to do." And he was right, because in a small group of equals consensus worked. On the whole Macartney-Snape and I tended to be more pushy, backed by Charlie's insistence that in Patagonia you can't sit around waiting for good weather—if any good weather does come it probably only lasts a day and you have to be up there, on the mountain, ready to go. Roskelley was the check to any impetuousness. A born hunter, full of tales of stalking bears and deer in the forests of Washington, on the mountain he reverses roles, becoming the prey, every sense acutely tuned to potential danger. Now in his mid-forties, his life seems to be focussed increasingly on home—on family and community, on his voluntary work with the fire service and on his zealous concern for the local environment; he isn't going to risk all that for any mountain.

We were reminded soon enough that even a comparatively simple mountain like Sarmiento can be dangerous. A day came, after three long trips carrying loads across the bridge and up steep slopes to the rocky platform of Camp One, when there was enough visibility to allow us onto the Southwest Ridge above.

It was only a rocky scramble, followed by an easy-angled glacier slope, but for me it was a symbolic moment when we reached the ice and stopped to put on crampons. Those steel spikes symbolised more than anything else my return to the world of high mountain glaciers. The last time I had worn them, three years earlier, they had dangled uselessly by their ankle straps, wrenched from my boots as I hurtled eighty metres down the precipitous flank of Panch Chuli V—a remote peak in the Indian Himalaya. By some miracle I had survived the fall, but I had broken my left ankle and badly smashed my right knee. It had been a long slow struggle to get back to the mountains and now, three years later, bending forward to ease my left boot into the crampon, I noticed the incongruous gleam of sharp new metal amidst rusty burrs and remembered that it was a replacement section: during the fall one spike of hard-forged steel had bent through ninety degrees as my foot hammered into granite. That graphic reminder should perhaps have filled me with dread but now there was not fear—rather a nervousness about how I would perform alongside my companions. Would I enjoy my climb or would it would turn out to be the drab postscript to a finished career?

The slope was not steep but in places the snow crust had melted away to reveal hard polished ice. Sudden gusts of wind came blasting, unannounced, across the ridge, threatening to catch us off balance, and we had to move carefully, ice axes ready to check any slip. My momentary nervousness was lost in concentration and I began to enjoy the steady rhythm and the reassuring sound of steel biting into ice. Like skiing or playing the piano after a long layoff, it felt right, with old familiar reflexes quickly returning.

After a couple of hours we reached a good site for our top camp—a deep bank of snow tucked in the lee of a rocky outcrop, sheltered from the prevailing westerly wind. The plan was to leave food and spare gear here, and return the next day with the largest tent. First we had to excavate a tent platform. Half an hour later, still immersed in practicalities, the five of us were hacking away with ice axes and shovels, when someone shouted and we all looked up to see the clouds swirling up and away to reveal, at last, the twin crystalline summits of Sarmiento, luminous in the sky, three thousand feet above us.

This was what I had really come for—this theatrical transformation scene, this transcendental moment of revelation, earned by hard patient slog. Suddenly we all talked at once, throwing opinions back and forth, arguing different routes, trying to gauge scale and steepness, but all agreeing that this mystery mountain had been worth all the effort of reaching.

Charlie, Tim and I lingered to savour this precious luminous scene while the other two set off down, and it was only when we returned to Camp One that we heard about the accident. Wickwire had been descending easy terrain, unroped. Suddenly, without warning, at the precise vulnerable moment when he was lifting one foot, a particularly violent gust of wind had caught him off balance and flung him through the air. He had landed on a sheet of ice, spun out of control and crashed feet first into a pile of boulders, badly spraining his right ankle. He had managed to hobble painfully down to the camp but now, as five of us gathered for supper in the communal tent, he admitted sadly that he would have to abandon the climb.

When we said good-bye to Wickwire the next morning he did not expect to see us again for two or three days. But by evening we were back, this time with a more serious casualty. Roskelley and Macartney-Snape were already at Camp Two when this accident happened. I had nearly reached the camp when I heard Charlie shouting below me. I turned round to see him crouched motionless on the ice. I couldn't hear any words above the noise of the wind so I descended a little and began to catch the word "arm." Just to make quite sure I climbed down closer. He was kneeling on the ice, clutching his right arm and grimacing with pain. "I've dislocated my shoulder. Get the others and tell them to bring a rope."

By the time we were all back with him, Porter was shivering and in shock. But he remained garrulous as ever as we escorted him down, furious with himself for letting the wind catch him out, apologising to us for the nuisance. Halfway down, safely off the ice, we stopped to inspect the damage. Roskelley, a trained paramedic, insisted that we should try and put the shoulder back as soon as possible, before it seized up completely. We should ideally have done it then and there, but we needed somewhere flat and dry, out of the wind, so Porter's shoulder had to wait until we were back with Wickwire at Camp One.

It was like being in the labour room and I wanted nothing to do with all that pain. I looked the other way, concentrating on cooking the supper, while Wickwire held Porter down on the tent floor, only mildly sedated with codeine, and the other two tried repeatedly to wrench his arm back into position. After about fifteen agonising attempts, Porter begged for relief and everyone rested while I served up supper. After the meal, Macartney-Snape, who had once been taught how to put a shoulder back in a remote bush hospital, asked to give Charlie's one more try. This time I had to assist in the torture chamber, adding more weight to immobilise the victim. I held down Porter's head and shoulders. He chewed on a piece of beef jerky and dug his fingernails into the left leg of Wickwire, who sat on his hips. Roskelley and Macartney-Snape stood over him, repeatedly pulling with all their might on the arm, sweating and gasping with the effort, as they tried to rotate the shoulder joint back into its socket.

After a while it grew cold and Roskelley said, "Wait a minute, I'm just going to get up and close that door." At which we all burst out laughing, envisaging some stranger peering in at the weird spectacle of five grown men grappling with each other in the semidarkness, one of them screaming through his teeth as he chewed frantically on the pink, pulpy remains of dried beef. The laughter gave us strength for more attempts but eventually, after wrestling for over an hour, Macartney-Snape announced, "I can't do it. You can rest now, Charlie." It was now several hours since the accident and the muscles round the joint had seized up completely. He needed expert help at the nearest hospital which was ninety miles to the north in Punta Arenas.

My reaction to the second accident was a selfish one: I was bitterly disappointed that it had probably spelt the end of our hopes for the summit. Wickwire was more magnanimous. Firstly, he insisted on carrying down a full load, hobbling painfully on his sprained ankle; secondly, he was determined that, even if he had lost his chance, *someone* should climb the mountain, putting the official stamp of success on the expedition which he had worked so hard to organise. Back at the boat, while Minos cooked up a hurried meal, Jim persuaded Charlie that he and Minos could crew for the one-armed skipper, crossing the Magellan Strait that night and reaching hospital the next day. The old sea dog stomped round the cabin, clutching his bundled-up, distorted arm in an old jacket, muttering into his beard about wanting a bigger crew. "I really need Tim," he said. The Stooges said nothing. I said nothing. Tim appeared to do nothing but afterwards he said, "I gave Charlie a quick hard look."

It obviously did the trick, because the skipper agreed to sail with a crew of just two, leaving Macartney-Snape, Roskelley and I with just enough time for one crack at the summit. Wickwire promised to return, in some boat or other, within five days. Roskelley was not entirely convinced and, as the three of us paddled back ashore to base camp that night, he muttered darkly, "We're marooned, stranded. I hate being away from the sound of an internal combustion engine." Less cynical, I found it deeply moving: *Gondwana* chugging away, navigation lights fading north into the dusk as we slid silently back to shore, staring ahead at Sarmiento, the whole mountain visible for the first time, orange in a violet sky.

Of course it was raining again in the morning and the wily old fox, Roskelley, tried to persuade us to be sensible, but we bullied him back up to Camp One and the following day, in equally squally weather, fought our way up to Camp Two, to lash down our dome tent on the platform we had prepared four days earlier. We spent a contented, domestic sort of evening in the tent. Macartney-Snape cooked supper while Roskelley argued the basic right of the American citizen to carry firearms. Then we drifted asleep in our cocoons of goose down, trying to ignore the battering of the wind on the tent.

The wind howled to a climax in the early hours of Wednesday then died down at dawn. As we left, pink light suffused diaphanous clouds, dispersing rapidly beneath us. I dared to hope that we were going to be lucky and, sure enough, as the day brightened to luminous tranquillity I realized that we had been given a wonderful gift. Only two things marred it. First, Charlie and Jim should have been there; second, we had to abandon hopes for the slightly higher East Summit, untrodden since 1956. To reach Mauri's route from this side would have meant traversing right through a zone of avalanche debris and when Roskelley stopped in front of it, with his look of deliberate purposefulness, I knew that there was no point in arguing. My feeling—and I think Tim's—was that you have occasionally to hurry past nasty places, but Roskelley was adamant that there should be no unnecessary risk. The man who had climbed K2 with Jim back in 1978—and followed that with a succession of brilliant Himalayan successes—was not going to take any chances on Sarmiento. So we opted for a shorter, safer new route up the South-West Face of the West Summit.

It was a pleasure to climb with two superlative mountaineers—both a hundred percent alert, concentrated and always following the safest line, seeking out islands of solid ice amidst suspicious slopes of windblown snow. In the shade, on the south side, there was little freeze-thaw and the choice lay between deep powder or rime-encrusted ice. Whenever possible we stuck to the latter, relishing the joy of crampon and axes sinking effortlessly into purpose-built Styrofoam.

It was wonderful to be ice climbing again for the first time in three years and, as my initial nervousness evaporated, I thought, "Why should they do all the leading?" Overawed by the others' experience, I had let them take turns in front, but now, towards the top of the South Face, as our summit came into view, I said, "Do you mind if I lead for a bit?" Above us was a steep ice gully which promised be the most exciting part of the climb, but to reach it we would have to wade through a long tedious snowfield. Macartney-Snape, ever the gentleman, suggested, "Why don't I break trail for a bit, then you can lead the interesting bit higher up." For "interesting" read steep, technical, absorbing. But I insisted, "No, thank you, I'll take over here. It's time I did some trail breaking. I can't have you colonials doing all the work." Self-esteem had to be assuaged and, after taking the end of the rope from Roskelley, it was good to throw myself into the hard labour of kicking through deep powder, panting hard, and doing a little jump each time I had to lift up my still imperfectly bending right knee.

The reward for all that hard slog was the final series of ice walls up the gully—real climbing, stepping up almost vertically, poised on just the front points of my crampons, with the whole three thousand feet of the South Face now dropping beneath me, and below that the fractured glacier tumbling far down into the red and green tapestry of the forest. Above me the gully emerged onto a gangway beneath the giant overhang of the summit. This gangway was the final question mark and we hoped desperately that it would coincide with a little notch we had spotted in the summit bulge.

Macartney-Snape led up the gangway. Roskelley followed, then the rope came tight and it was my turn. The summit overhang was now leaning right out over me—a giant, two-hundred-foot-high mushroom, hanging thirty feet out in space, encrusted with swirling, crystalline feathers of rime—but, as we had hoped, the gangway led right up underneath it to a notch, where the other two now stood silhouetted against the sky.

From the notch it was an easy walk to the top of the mushroom, which we reached at three o'clock in the afternoon. The sun shone and the air was miraculously still. I was reminded of a fine winter's day in Scotland. There was the same intricate, glittering pattern of mountain and sea, but on a grander scale, with huge glaciers and icecaps and the wonderfully surreal rime battlements of our own mountain, Sarmiento, to remind me that we were in Tierra del Fuego, suspended between Atlantic and Pacific, at "the uttermost ends of the earth."

Forty minutes passed all too quickly, then it was time to descend, hurried down by Roskelley who was rightly anxious to descend as far as possible before the light faded. His urgency was vindicated soon after dark when the wind returned suddenly, without warning, transforming our benign face of Sarmiento into a hideous maelstrom of spindrift, pouring down relentlessly on our heads, stinging eyeballs raw. It seemed that every one of the billion tiny granules of snow on the mountain was being funnelled deliberately, malignantly onto our heads, down our necks and into our mittens every time we took them off to fumble with abseil brakes. We were being forced to pay for our summit gift, and if we failed to find our way off the mountain, we would have to spend the whole night out in this smothering icy torrent. I was very glad that Roskelley, without my impediment of lousy eyesight, was going first, ropelength by ropelength, finding the way out of this hell hole.

There were moments, suspended on the rappel ropes in the swirling blackness, when I thought of that other descent in the dark, three years earlier on Panch Chuli, when the peg came out. The terrain here was different, with no jagged rocks. I wondered whether one might even survive a fall to the foot of the face, then remembered all those ice bulges we had climbed that morning and imagined graphically the life being pounded from my body. Each time I set off down the ropes, I couldn't help glancing anxiously at the anchor, just to reassure myself that it was sound. In fact they were bomb-proof, and my fear, like most fear, was irrational. Most of the time I was far too busy to be frightened. As always on these occasions, there was a grim satisfaction in coping efficiently, concentrating one hundred percent, keeping discomfort to a minimum. It was horrible, but the whole unpleasant episode only lasted two hours and by nine o'clock we were back in the tent, congratulating ourselves on our fantastic luck, as the roar of the MSR stove challenged the noise of wind outside.

Packing up the tent on Thursday morning, Macartney-Snape and I told Roskelley to get inside and hold it down while we untied it from its moorings. A moment later Roskelley's hand shot out of the door and grabbed a piton as the wind picked up him and tent, threatening to fling them both over the edge. He looked at us suspiciously and said, "I don't wanna seem like an old fuddy-duddy or anything, but I really think we should rope together down to Camp One." So we roped up for slopes less than thirty degrees, clawing our way horizontally on hands and knees, like a replay of the famous Python sketch of people climbing the pavement. It looked very silly, but I was extremely glad of the security. Two accidents had been unlucky; a third would have looked careless.

Two days later Macartney-Snape and I did the final load-carry down from Camp One, while Roskelley cleared up base camp. The loads were heavy and my bad knee twinged uncomfortably on the final slog through the bog, lurching from hummock to hummock, struggling to keep up with Tim's effortless stride. It was another typical damp overcast afternoon, but the bog seemed more luminous than ever—orange, yellow, crimson and green, with brilliant white lichen encrusted like coral on the skeletal remains of long-dead trees. I had to admit to myself that the beauty of it all was enhanced by success. It had been wonderful to live for three weeks in this enchanted landscape but, as always, I needed the simple satisfaction of a job completed, a goal attained. That fulfillment was reinforced when we tramped into base camp to discover that Roskelley had cleared away every trace of our stay and was waiting for us on the beach, listening delightedly to the deep throb of a diesel engine. A hundred yards offshore, a Chilean fishing boat rocked in the swell and, as we were rowed out to meet it, we could see from the smile on his face that Jim Wickwire, despite his own bad luck, was also pleased with our eleventh hour success on Sarmiento.

The Longest Cave

Roger W. Brucker and Richard A. Watson

Editors' note: Roger Brucker is an American cave explorer and the author and coauthor of five books about caves. He is best known for his exploration of Kentucky's Mammoth Cave system and began exploring sections of it in 1954. Mammoth Cave is the world's longest explored cave system, and Brucker and his friends are credited with many of the most significant finds. The excerpt below is from The Longest Cave *(1976) by Brucker and Richard A. Watson.*

Author's note: Mammoth Cave in Kentucky is 404 miles long and still growing through survey and exploration. It is three times longer than any other cave. The following story tells of a breakthrough set of discoveries that taught the explorers to "follow the water" to find natural connections between the big caves. These trips revealed the clues necessary to connect Crystal Cave, Unknown Cave, Salts Cave, Colossal Cave, and finally Mammoth Cave in 1972.

Soon after Roger Brucker unveiled his map of the lower levels of Crystal Cave in Flint Ridge, Bill Austin recognized from the maps and descriptions that Jack Lehrgerger, Russ Gurnee, and Roy Charlton—who had been sent out to explore around Bogardus Waterfall—had actually gone to another place, subsequently named Bogus Bogardus Waterfall. This left a passage still to be explored at Bogardus Waterfall. If it went, it might connect

Crystal Cave with Salts Cave. So in July 1954 Bill, Jack, Roger, Phil, and Dixon Brackett took a grinding eighteen-hour trip into the Bogardus area to straighten out the ambiguities of the C-3 expedition map.

The explorers proceeded to the real Bogardus Waterfall. Nearby was an entrance to a small passage over which the words "A NICE CRAWL" had been written in soot with the flame of a carbide lamp. Bill said he had written them in 1948 when he was exploring with Jim Dyer, and that the passage went a long way. He had turned back at a pit. There would be plenty for everyone out there, he said, so he, Jack, and Phil crawled on their bellies into the small passage. Roger, after his long drive from Ohio to Kentucky, was beginning to feel the effects of lack of sleep, so he decided to take a nap while the others explored. Dixon stayed with him. They slept for several hours, awaking when they heard a shout. The others had found their way to the bottom of Bogus Bogardus Waterfall by a new route. Roger fired up his carbide lamp and crawled down through a muddy, tight tube to the others. Dixon followed. By this time the advance party was ready for a meal.

Bill and Jack had taken a long crawl leading to a small elliptical tube with a sandy floor that took them to a cluster of dry vertical shafts. Then they followed another crawlway, but abandoned it to crawl through a small side passage back into the Bogardus Waterfall Trail. The crawlway they had abandoned was still unexplored. Roger asked how to find it. Jack pointed across the stone lily pads at the entrance to an ocher-colored tube just big enough to slide into. While the others were eating, Roger crawled off to explore.

Out of sight and hearing of the others, Roger found the passage getting smaller. Grape and small crystals on the walls, ceiling, and floor tore at his clothing—which is why they named it Fishhook Crawl—and he tensed as he realized he would have to back out of the passage if he could not find a place to turn around. He decided he must have missed the side passage that led back to Bogardus Waterfall Trail. There were no scuff marks on the floor. The passage ahead was virgin.

He decided to go around one more corner. Wham! As he stuck his head around the corner, a cold breeze struck him squarely in the face. It came from a black hole that had appeared at the end of the tunnel. The passage was even smaller ahead. Roger's adrenaline surged as he pushed rapidly ahead on his belly. The breeze felt like a gale. The hole, however, was a deception. It was just another bend in the passage. So were the next several holes. Then, after about 400 feet of very tight belly crawling, Roger thrust his head out a tiny window-like opening into a pit about ten feet in diameter, with a basin floor ten feet below. The pit was decorated with brownish-black flowstone, so Roger named it Black Onyx Pit. Above the window the walls ballooned out.

Roger could not turn around, or even roll over on his back in the tiny crawlway. But if he could get out of the window and get up onto a ledge a few feet to left on the wall of Black Onyx Pit, he could see what he had found, and could turn around for the long crawl back. He had to push his body out into empty space until he could bend sideways at the waist. Then, holding on to the slick cave onyx projections at the level of the hole, he slid his legs out and down the wall into a layback against the wall. The traverse across the side wall to the ledge was not difficult. He did not think getting back to the window would be easy, but he was sure he could do it.

The ledge was a delight. It led to an extension of Black Onyx Pit that was nearly thirty feet long, eighteen feet wide, and fifty feet high. Peering into the gloom, he could see several leads, including the entrance to a passage five feet in diameter that departed from one wall. He could do nothing more now, however, for he had overstayed his time and the others would be expecting him. He climbed back over to the window.

The window in the wall of Black Onyx Pit leading back into Fishhook Crawl was not easy to enter. Roger put his arms into the opening and hung there, his feet swinging free, but the hole was not large enough for him to pull himself up by his arms and at the same time bend his head and shoulders into it. Finally he had to reverse his entrance procedure, pulling his body up in a layback on the slippery wall until he could slide his head and shoulders sideways into the hole. Then, with his arms outstretched down the passage and his shoulders wedged, he flailed his legs in the open air of Black Onyx Pit until he managed to slide forward into Fishhook Crawl on his belly. Then he slid forward like a snake in a hurry toward Bogardus Waterfall. When he was nearly there, he heard Jack calling him. He answered elatedly. Jack listened to his account, and then went off down Fishhook Crawl. He checked Roger's Black Onyx Pit, and came back smiling.

The breakthrough into a new passage complex of Crystal Cave in the heart of Flint Ridge had been made. Later it was learned that during the C-3 expedition a crucial crawlway opening along the line of discovery had not been found because during an exploration-trip rest stop Russ Gurnee had sat his six-foot-five-inch frame on the ledge above it, hiding it completely. Now, however, the way was clear. They planned a Thanksgiving expedition to explore the passages leading off from Black Onyx Pit. It would be a big job, and there was some discussion about personnel.

Red Watson had joined the ROTC during the Korean War to avoid the draft. The war was over by the time he got his commission. He spent a year in Denver going to an Air Force aerial-photography school, and then was sent to an air base outside Columbus, Ohio. Searching for outdoor adventure, he looked through the membership list of the National Speleological Society for the member in Columbus who had the lowest NSS number, and who thus would have been an NSS member longer than any of the others.

Jim Dyer answered the phone and after listening awhile said, "You call Phil Smith."

Phil was working on his thesis for an MA in educational psychology at The Ohio State University, but he told Red to come on over anyway. Red climbed up to a room under the eves of an old house where slanted ceilings forced tall Phil to stoop except in the center of the room. The room was piled with books, papers, and camera equipment. On the walls were cave maps, and photographs of caves and of scenes from Shakespearean plays.

Red and Phil talked, sizing each other up. Phil stretched out lazily in a chair, his legs crossed at the ankles, has hands clasped, flesh spare on his lanky frame. Red roamed the room, looking at everything, his compact body full of nervous energy.

"Have you done much caving?" Phil asked.

"Some," Red said.

"Our caving is pretty strenuous," Phil went on.

Red changed the subject to mountain climbing. He had done some climbing, but did not want to mention that he had been in only four caves in his life, one of which was almost 100 yards long, and another of which was Carlsbad Caverns on a commercial tour. The other two did not amount to much.

Four hours later Phil and Red had discussed if not solved most of the world's major problems, and Red left with an invitation to go with Phil to his home in Springfield, Ohio, for Thanksgiving dinner. Then they would go to Floyd Collins' Crystal Cave for a big trip in Flint Ridge. Red stumbled down the stairs, glancing at the magazines Phil had given him. He read through the rest of the night. In the *Louisville Courier-Journal Magazine*, an extensive feature article emphasized the danger of getting lost while exploring caves. Red wondered whether Phil knew Crystal Cave well enough not to get lost. "Seven Days in the Hole" by Robert Halmi, reporting in *True Magazine* on the C-3 expedition, filled Red with visions of the horror of the Keyhole, Bottomless Pit, and Formerly

Impossible. He slept fitfully, cave darkness terrifying his dreams. He awoke around noon, and never thereafter was he so frightened of caving as he was before ever going caving at all. The reality of those dreaded places came as a welcomed relief when he actually experienced them in Crystal Cave.

Phil outfitted Red with caving gear, and lectured about caving on the long ride from Ohio to Kentucky. Red listened carefully, cramming, a bit anxious because he thought everyone took him to be an experienced caver. In fact, he had not fooled Phil, and he was wrong in thinking that he had to be an experienced caver to join the Flint Ridge Crew. When Jim Dyer had suggested to Phil the need to develop teams of explorers, Jim had also remarked that desire and fitness were as important as previous caving experience. Red was Phil's first green recruit.

In turn, Red had fastened on Phil as the one he should follow to learn. However, when he reached Flint Ridge, Red began to get confused. He had thought that Phil was the organizing force behind this expedition. Then he met Roger Brucker, who seemed to view the expedition as part of his cartography program. However, Bill Austin, manager of Crystal Cave, was directing operations. And underground, on the long crawl out to the Bogardus area, Red found some of the cavers deferring to Jack Lehrberger, who charismatically projected the image of being the biggest daddy cave explorer of them all. The amazing thing was that there was no conflict in these crisscrossing lines.

Phil was busily managing, an occupation that led him three years later to found the Cave Research Foundation. Roger Brucker was constructing maps, and would become the first Chief Cartographer for the Flint Ridge Cave System. Bill was an heir to the finest cave system in the world—Floyd Collins' Crystal Cave—and he was protective of his property. Jack, most interested in exploration, was quietly eager to go beyond the limits of previous penetration in Flint Ridge. Roger McClure, Dave Jones, Jack Reccius, Bill

Hulstrunk, Dixon Brackett, Bob White, and Red Watson—only seven Indians for four chiefs—followed the low passage on hands and knees, obeying orders. Red crawled blindly, because he soon saw that he could not memorize the complicated route back as he had read in a book that he should. He was dependent on the others.

During the C-3 expedition, heavy-duty phone wire had been laid from the Austins' yard where the Headquarters tent was located on the surface of Flint Ridge to the Lost Passage in Crystal Cave underground. The heavy wire and field telephones had taken so much energy to install that Dave Jones, who was a recording engineer, adapted lightweight, sound-powered telephones for use in Crystal Cave. One could both listen and speak through a single crystal earphone that could be clipped anywhere along a thin, plastic-covered wire. A thousand feet of this wire weighed only a few pounds. At Floyd's Lost Passage, Dave spliced one of the rolls into the heavy telephone line. Transmission was loud and clear. Jacque Austin on the surface expressed suitably serious interest in the continuously reported accomplishments as the explorers unrolled the wire toward Bogardus Waterfall.

When the end of the previous survey was reached, Roger Brucker assigned segments of the passage ahead to various teams of surveyors. After five hours the new route had been surveyed all the way to Black Onyx Pit.

Meanwhile, Phil and Bill had gone beyond Black Onyx Pit to make a stupendous discovery. Instead of going up onto the ledge Roger had found to explore the high leads, they decided to continue through a crack at the bottom of Black Onyx Pit. It was Bill's experience that such drain passages often lead to larger passages. Within twenty feet they came to another drop, a much larger and deeper part of Black Onyx Pit. Phil uncoiled a shining new white nylon rope that contrasted with the muddy explorers. He tied the rope to a rock projection to use as a hand line for the climb down.

The passage continued on the other side of the pit as a canyon thirty feet high and five to ten feet wide, with possible routes of travel on several levels. Phil explored a small side passage while Bill went on down the main canyon. Coming back from the side passage, Phil decided to go back to the roped pit to leave a note for the surveyors who would be coming along. Bill and Phil were only fifty feet beyond the previously known limits, but already there were so many leads to choose from that the follow-up teams would need clear guidance.

Then Phil followed Bill's scuff marks over large boulders jammed in the canyon passage.

"Come up here and look at this!" Bill shouted.

Phil rushed on to find Bill standing on the edge of the biggest pit either had ever seen. They called the wide platform they stood on the Balcony, and the pit itself the Overlook. Their lights neither reached the ceiling nor the floor of the pit in front of them. Its far wall was nearly fifty feet away. They threw a rock. Several seconds later it splashed in a deep pool. They estimated that the Overlook had a total height of about 150 feet. Phil and Bill were standing on the Balcony about sixty feet above its bottom.

This discovery spurred them on. There were at least three obvious leads off the Balcony of the Overlook.

They chose a passage opening behind a spray of water on the same level as the entry passage. A few minutes after ducking through the shower, they came to a junction. In one direction a canyon led down to a rectangular passage four feet wide and six feet high. It offered more of the same wet and muddy prospect. The passage straight ahead was somewhat smaller, but it showed a sprinkling of gypsum on the walls, a sandy floor, and a change in the texture of the rock itself.

The choice was obvious. At Bogus Bogardus Waterfall the explorers had gone down to lower, wetter cave. Fishhook Crawl, Black Onyx Pit, and the passages beyond the Overlook were also low. They had gone deep into the depths of Crystal Cave. To find big, dry passages higher up under Flint Ridge, perhaps without any direct surface entrance, they would have to climb back up again. Cave passages on higher levels are often characterized by growths of gypsum crystals on their walls. When Bill saw the sparkling of gypsum in the passage before him, he was as pleased as he had been when he found the Overlook. Behind him, Phil was certain that this was the way to connect Crystal Cave with Salts Cave.

They walked rapidly into the passage, then crouched. Finally, when they were forced to their bellies by the lowering ceiling, Bill, in the lead, turned a disgusted look back to Phil.

"Oh, hell!" Phil said, and started backing out.

Back at the junction again, they climbed down into the wet passage. Phil was overheated from the crawlway. He was also already somewhat uneasy about having turned back, because the gypsum crawl did go on. It still does, unexplored.

The wet passage Phil and Bill now ran down got to be ten feet wide and seven feet high in places. It kept its rectangular shape, and it trended distinctly downward. They had very early along named it Storm Sewer.

After several hundred feet the ceiling closed down until they were crawling through mud and water in a passage three feet high and ten feet wide. The persistent rectangular cross-section was so striking that the tunnel seemed man-made. A thin layer of mud covered the ceiling, walls, and floor. They knew they were getting down near the base-level of the Green River, which was known to backflood from the surface into the cave passages for thousands of feet and as high as fifty or sixty feet above normal river level.

"What's the weather like outside?" Phil asked.

"I haven't the foggiest," Bill replied.

This base-level caving was something new to Bill and Phil. They had never gotten this low under Flint Ridge before.

After a quarter of a mile Storm Sewer opened into a large passage making a T-junction. It was as though they had now entered the master sewer, with a vaulted limestone ceiling stretching six feet over a mud-bank floor twenty to thirty feet wide. A few hundred feet to the right, the room closed down to a muddy crater with no opening at the bottom. To the left, the big passage contained a small stream that flowed in a mud-walled canyon. Passage walls were twenty feet apart, with a fifteen-foot ceiling. Bill slid fifteen feet down a mud bank to the water on his feet, twisted back, and almost fell, crying, "Blindfish!"

All of these discoveries seemed to offer names immediately. The passage was named Eyeless Fish Trail, and the river it contained, Eyeless Fish River. The river was a major discovery that culminated years of exploration in Floyd Collins' Crystal Cave. This small stream was surely part of a large underground river system that extended at near base level beneath all the caves of Flint Ridge. If they could follow it, they would surely connect all the Flint Ridge caves into one system. Eyeless Fish River might even extend under Houchins Valley, which separated Flint Ridge from Mammoth Cave Ridge. The blindfish in Eyeless Fish Trail of Crystal Cave might be able to swim all the way to Mammoth Cave. But even if they could, this would be no promise that cavers—obeying the rule that you should follow the water to find new caves—actually could follow. Underground rivers have a tendency to siphon—that is, the ceilings of the passages that contain them sometimes meet the surface of the water, making it virtually impossible for the explorers to go on. Siphons are formidable barriers to exploration even for cavers with special diving equipment, and there is never any guarantee that the ceiling will rise into open air beyond.

Downstream, the water of Eyeless Fish River flowed into a narrow black opening. At this level, so close to the Green River outside, it would probably soon siphon. Even if it did not siphon, it would be very difficult to follow. Bill and Phil decided to explore upstream. Eyeless Fish River might intersect the bottoms of pits up which they could climb into unknown higher-level passages.

They sloshed upstream until the roof of Eyeless Fish River dipped down so that further progress would have required crawling in the water. Here they traced their initials, "P.M.S." and "B.A.," in the mud, and turned back. In a few hours they had found more new cave passages in Crystal Cave than half a hundred explorers had during the previous thirty years. On the way out, Phil sank to his crotch in the mud trying to climb up the bank of Eyeless Fish Trail. He noted that the mud out that way constituted a hazard.

It was not only the mud that was dangerous. A few years later Bill, Roger Brucker, and Dave Jones took two top adventure journalists—Coles Phinizy and Robert Halmi of *Sports Illustrated*—to see Eyeless Fish Trail. The water was up, and at one point a foot-wide bridge of mud crossed the river with a dark pool of water lying on either side. Bill walked across, with Phinizy, Halmi, and Jones following. Roger, however, had slung around his neck a steel ammunition case full of Bill's camera equipment. He decided, for safety's sake, to crawl on his hands and knees across the bridge. Sliding slowly down the mud bank on all fours, he slid smoothly off and head first into a pool about two feet in diameter on one side of the bridge. He went completely under, turned over, and came up banging his head solidly on a ledge underwater. The river ordinarily flowed on a level about six feet lower than it was now, and Roger knew there were passages down at that level into which he could be swept. He floundered wildly in a long moment of panic. He could not breathe. He was totally submerged in cold water, suspended in total darkness. There was nothing for his hands and feet to get a purchase on. Then his arms and head emerged back out the opening.

"Help!"

Bill had already raced back down the mud bank and was crouching on the bridge, extending a hand to Roger. "Taking a bath?" he asked, as he grabbed Roger firmly by a wrist.

The steel ammunition case also popped to the surface and was retrieved. Bill showed great satisfaction with the fact that the camera equipment he had packed emerged from the experience safe and dry. Roger emerged safe, but he was very wet. At a supply dump on the way out of the cave, Dave ran a butane torch over Roger, raising clouds of steam from his clothing. Despite this, it was a long, cold trip for Roger from Eyeless Fish Trail to the Crystal Entrance.

On the original discovery trip, Bill and Phil returned from Eyeless Fish Trail to Black Onyx Pit to find Jack Lehrberger and Dixon Brackett exploring leads in that vicinity. Roger Brucker was supposed to meet them there, but the surveying had taken longer than they had expected. Always impatient with delays, Phil was furious. There was so much to be done. Then the surveying parties began catching up with the explorers. Everyone was so excited at the descriptions of the new finds that Bill and Phil immediately guided some of the surveyors to the Overlook. The rest of the party laid the telephone line into a side pit, a dark, elongated room six or eight feet wide with a forty-foot ceiling. Only the lights made it seem like a camp. This dismal place was fittingly named Camp Pit.

At the Overlook there ensued a great rock-throwing orgy. In a few minutes all the larger loose rocks on the Balcony—no more than ten or twelve—had been pitched over, with enormously satisfying results. Each time, a long silence was followed by a deep, heavy *ker-chunk* from the pool of water far below. Nothing was left except a huge block of limestone about six feet long, three feet wide, and three feet high, seemingly just teetering on the edge of the Balcony. By this time Jack Reccius, a caver from Louisville who had done a lot of exploring in Salts Cave and Unknown Cave with Jack Lehrberger, was wild with enthusiasm. He rushed to the edge of the pit without thought of life or limb to strain at the block of limestone.

"Help me, help me!" he yelled. Several people tried, gingerly, to pry the block over the edge without going over themselves. Others were not about to join the madmen. Red crouched back against the wall of the Balcony, well away from the edge of the Overlook. He had gone along with everything so far, but did not want to get close to the edge of that deep pit. The boulder won. Twenty-two years later it is still as solidly attached—and as precarious-looking—on the edge of the Overlook Balcony as it has probably been for hundreds, if not thousands, of years.

The pitch of excitement could not be subdued. Bill and Phil led some of the party on out Storm Sewer to see the blindfish in Eyeless Fish River. On the way back they stopped at a walking lead, a broad opening ten feet high by five feet wide in the side of Storm Sewer.

"Red," Phil shouted, "this one's for you! Explore some virgin cave."

The others stood back expectantly as Red ducked forward. He had done all right so far as part of a survey team. Now the lies had caught up with him, and he felt as though he had told a group of climbers that he could climb when he never had before, and then found himself forced into leading up a vertical wall.

"We'll wait here," Phil said, slumping down to sit with his back against the wall of Storm Sewer. The others sat down, too.

Not only had Red never explored virgin cave before, he had to go alone. His body carried him along. A few feet into the passage, he stepped down and turned a corner. There in front of him was a blank wall. It was not a pile of breakdown blocks, nor a mud fill blocking the passage. It was a solid stone wall. For a moment he thought he had been tricked, but, no, he had noticed quite carefully that there had been no tracks on the floor. Phil had not set it up for him.

"It ends!" Red shouted back.

There were sounds of disbelief and disgust from Storm Sewer. Groaning, the others got up to set the newcomer straight. They walked around the corner and stared for a moment in disbelief. So much new cave had been discovered on this trip that everyone expected every passage to go and go. Then they all burst out in laughter. Phil could say nothing because he was choking, so he just pounded Red on the back. Back out into Storm Sewer, Phil wrote over the top of the arched opening in big letters with the flame of his carbide lamp: "WATSON'S FOLLY." That seemed a little hardhearted to Red at the time.

It had been a hard trip for everyone. Some people in the party had complained about the difficulty on the way in, and had several times suggested that the group turn back. After reaching Camp Pit, one person refused to go a few hundred feet farther down the passage to see the Overlook. Three of the party members never entered Floyd Collins' Crystal Cave again after this trip.

For others, this discovery trip was the beginning of Flint Ridge caving. Jim Dyer's hypothesis and hope that Floyd Collins' Crystal Cave was the heart of a large Flint Ridge Cave System had been confirmed. For Phil and Roger, the discoveries proved the value of a kind of organized cave exploration they were developing in the Flint Ridge Reconnaissance, and that would lead to the founding of the Cave Research Foundation. For Red, it was the grandest adventure he had ever had. He had fallen in love with Floyd Collins' Crystal Cave.

Pyramid Peak, East Face

Chris Davenport

Editors' note: Chris Davenport is considered one of the best big moun-tain skiers of all time. In 1996 and 2001 he won the World Extreme Skiing Championships in Alaska. In 2011 Davenport and alpinist Neal Beidleman skied 2,000 feet of the Lhotse Face of Mount Ever-est, one of just a few descents of the Lhotse Face. Between January 22, 2006, and January 19, 2007, Davenport skied all fifty-four of Colo-rado's 14,000-foot peaks. This required an impressive combination of mountaineering and skiing skills, as well as the ability to predict weather patterns and snow conditions. Davenport and various com-panions faced everything from water ice to powder, beautiful sunny Colorado days to intense storms and freezing temperatures. Davenport climbed more than 200,000 vertical feet during the adventure and often faced treacherous descents with minimal snow cover. Colorado ski alpinist Lou Dawson was the first to climb and ski all fifty-four peaks. That took Dawson thirteen years—Davenport did it in one. And yet, Davenport's short piece here, about his favorite descent, the famed Landry Line on Pyramid Peak's east face, is fascinating for its brevity. Clearly, Davenport is a man of action, not words. His books include Ski the 14ers *and* 50 Classic Ski Descents of North America.

When Chris Landry completed the first ski descent of Pyramid Peak in April of 1978, he could not have know how "ahead of its time" this descent would come to be in the history of North American ski mountaineering. While descents of this magnitude were happening with some regularity in the Alps, only a few had been done on this side of the Atlantic, namely Bill Briggs's decent of the Grand Teton, Fritz Stammberger's descent of North Maroon Peak's North Face, and Sylvan Saudan's descent of the Newton-Clark Headwall on Mt. Hood, all of which took place in 1971. Landry went on to claim a stunning descent of the Liberty Ridge on Mt. Rainier in 1980, yet his Pyramid feat remained unrepeated for nearly twenty-eight years. This fact weighed heavy on my mind as I approached the upper East Face of Pyramid for the first time in April of 2006. Within the Colorado ski-mountaineering community the Landry line was certainly discussed during those interim years, and possibly attempted more than once, but it slowly gained a fearsome reputation by doing nothing else than just sitting there, beautiful, daunting, and un-skied. A virtual "glass-ceiling" had been created over one of the continent's most aesthetic ski lines, a ceiling that was ready to break.

Pyramid Peak's East Face is fairly unique within the realm of Colorado mountain topography. While Colorado can boast the most high peaks of any region in North America, it also has very high valleys, so rarely do the classic ski lines drop more than 3000 feet. The East Face rises 4400 feet abruptly out of the East Maroon Creek valley and only at the very bottom does the angle relent to under 40 degrees. 2000 feet up the line the face splits, with the regular East Face continuing directly up at a 45-degree angle to the summit ridge near 14,000 feet and the Landry Line peeling off through a short couloir and heading directly at 50-degrees-plus to the summit at 14,025 feet.

As I sat on the summit under brilliant blue skies and calm winds with my partners Ted and Neil, I couldn't help but wonder what thoughts had gone through Chris's mind as he and partner Michael Kennedy (who down-climbed the route) sat in that very position. Were they full of nervous energy as we were, or carefree and confident? Those two had been without the benefit of accurate avalanche and weather forecasting, and were skiing on the soft boots and long, skinny skis of the day. Whatever advantages we thought we might have had as modern ski-mountaineers did nothing to satiate our nerves and concerns. The first 100 feet of the line rolls off into the abyss, getting steeper and steeper until you're at the point where you wonder if this might be the steepest thing you have ever skied. But just as that thought crosses your mind, another interrupts it. This is the most awesome thing you have ever skied! People often ask me what my favorite 14er ski descent in Colorado is, and unfailingly I say, "Pyramid Peak's Landry Line!"

Khumbu Bound

Jonathan Waterman

Editors' note: As a wilderness-loving youth from a Boston suburb, Jon Waterman dreamed of expeditions to far-flung places. His interests led him to a new route on Mount Logan in the Yukon, a first ascent of Thelay Sagar in the Garwhal Himalaya, and a bold winter ascent of the Cassin Ridge on Alaska's Denali, where he thoroughly documented northern mountaineering with his books Surviving Denali, High Alaska *and* In the Shadow of Denali. *Disenchanted with conventional climbing, and increasingly interested in sharing the world through adventure travelogues, he adopted what he considered the ideal extended adventure model, epitomized by the British author Bill Tilman. Waterman began writing books that include* Kayaking the Vermilion Sea, *about environmental degradation in Mexico's Sea of Cortez observed during his two-month paddling journey;* A Most Hostile Mountain: Re-Creating the Duke of Abruzzi's Historic Expedition on Mount Saint Elias, *told from Waterman's five-month sailing and climbing epic; and* Arctic Crossing, *detailing Waterman's 2,200-mile, ten-month solo across the Northwest Passage. In 2008, supported by the National Geographic Society, he paddled the Colorado River from source to sea and shared his findings through a broad media campaign and his books* Running Dry *and* The Colorado River. *By tackling thorny environmental and cultural issues in narratives that transcend traditional adventure yarns, he has won numerous awards, including a Literature Fellowship from the National Endowment for the Arts, an Emmy, and the*

Sigurd F. Olson Nature Writing Award. Herein, from his "Khumbu Bound" article published in the Winter 1991 Summit *magazine, he describes Bill Tilman's 1950 reconnaissance of Everest.*

Two a.m., eastern Nepal.

I have become a human jack-in-the-box, and fingerlock the armrest to minimize airtime above my belt-less bus seat. Nonetheless, axle-deep ruts combined with a lack of shocks pops me out—I suffer four headshots with the ceiling. Exhaust fumes dull my thinking until dawn breaks outside the window. Typifying Nepal travel, I experience a blind man's rebirth: the misery of night is abandoned as I gape at the magical countryside.

The morning is alive with fly-chased people balancing water jugs on their heads, men holding other men's hands, a woman with blood-red bettle nut juice on her lips, smoking septuagenarians squatting in fields, and a boy with a machete chasing a squawking chicken. The people twinkle by too quickly to grasp, but the fertile green fields and dark dirt chocolate still stretch like infinity. I feel lucky for the freedom to have traveled halfway around the world while most Nepalese will only walk as far as their bare feet will endure the rough ground.

After several flat tires, Sherpa Tenje and I debark at a bazaar on the Terai plains. A man in rags holds out a wooden snake, intricately carved from wood. Fascinated, I look closer and he drops it in my hands. He demands 400 rupees.

"No," I say, "I can't afford your snake, but you've done a fine job."

"You are a wealthy American," he says, "but I will give you the snake for 390 rupees."

"No," I say, smiling. "In my country, I am not wealthy."

But the man shakes his head with great conviction. He waves his finger like a baton and wherever I go in Nepal, his reply will resonate: "You are wrong, Sir. You are very wealthy man."

I thank the man for his advice as my guide tows me toward a Russian-made bus enveloped in dirt and diesel soot, packed with people, chickens, and a pig. We squeeze in.

What initially seemed Tenje's shy demeanor is really his lack of English. Furthermore, my young companion doesn't seem to understand maps and is just as lost as I am. Although Tenje has never been to eastern Nepal, I have hired him for top Sherpa wages ($3.50 a day plus expenses) in an attempt to bridge a culture that might otherwise elude me.

I have another interest, dating back to 1950, when Oscar Houston was given permission to reconnoiter Mount Everest. His party drove from India to Dharan (accidentally meeting then inviting the legendary explorer Bill Tilman) to join their 175-mile walk to and climb of Everest. As the first Westerners to penetrate the southern flanks of Mount Everest, their trek foreshadowed the mountain tourism epoch that would profoundly impact Nepalese culture.

Over the years, Sherpas would learn new languages, adopt Western clothing, and return home from expeditions with wages beyond their dreams. Otherwise, foreign aid money poured in, so hospitals, schools, and roads were built. Finally, the deforestation in popular trekking areas accelerated, 8000-meter peak basecamps became trash dumps, farmers turned into shrewd lodge owners, lowly paid officials bowed to corruption, while the loyal Sherpas became serac targets and porter slaves for climbers from around the world.

During their expedition, Bill Tilman, Betsy Cowles, and Charlie and Oscar Houston debated whether the ensuing tourist industry would open a Pandora's Box of cultural problems or improve the Sherpa standard of living. Otherwise, they paved diplomatic paths for the successful ascent of Everest in 1953, as well as a subsequent flood of expeditions from around the world. But after 1952, a more direct route was found from Kathmandu, a road was built to Jiri, and an airport was constructed in Lukla that allowed climbers immediate access to the mountains. So with the exception of an occasional trekker, no Everest expeditions would follow Tilman's footsteps.

On the heels of explorers two generations removed, we stop in Dharan, and Tenje leads me to a restaurant. My baby-faced companion is replete with wall-to-wall Levi trekking garb and a high-buffed hairdo. Once inside, the Hindu music blares from a battered cassette deck with the amplified din of hundreds of mosquitoes. My ears ache, so I ask Tenje to politely ask the proprietor if he can turn the volume down. Tenje tries to process my English for a minute, then complies, shouting and gesturing in Nepalese at the owner, who smiles grandly, pops in Springsteen's "Born in the USA" and cranks the volume up even louder. It's not what I want, but I wave my thanks anyway.

While I cannot speak Nepalese, Tenje has picked up a great deal more English—nonetheless, such miscommunications are constant.

As I sip sweet tea, I try to imagine the Houstons and Tilman stumbling upon the hub-bub of Dharan, then hustling to the sanctity of the nearby mountains. But the years have wrought tremendous change, even here in the Third World, and where my predecessors once walked, there is now a road. Tenje procures an expensive taxi, but I insist on the bus, where we find room enough clinging to the roof rack.

The bus chugs up numerous switchbacks. Hundreds of terraced fields circle mountainsides like contour lines on a map. I am aghast to find no wasted acre of farming, even the steepest hillsides have been hand terraced, lovingly patted, manured, and wrested from the stony earth.

I am truly off guard here—which drew me to Nepal to begin with. I am assaulted by colors and textures and broad smiling faces that my wildest suburb-weaned fantasies could not conceive. I back off from smells that would make a New York City bag-lady gag. Consequently, in my loneliness and lack of communicable companionship, and through the void of a singular challenging objective (a mountain expedition) on which I can sate myself, I turn critical.

Our Western society is a soft place indeed, a full universe away from the immutable harshness of Nepal living. Yet it is not my first time in Asia, and understanding Nepal will mean seeing this country through its eyes rather than my own. It will be a challenge the equal of any obstacle on the trail ahead.

Black smoke pours from the muffler, schoolboys shout from the road, a girl vomits from the window. Finally, several thousand feet above Dharan, we arrive at Dhankhuta.

In 1950 Cowles wrote, "The dream town of all our lives. Imagine to yourself a clean, happy, prosperous village, built with taste and style, beautifully situated on a ridge where poinsettia and bohinnia trees are in bloom. Its streets are swept twice daily, and its houses replastered twice yearly. . . .

"None of us will forget Dhankhuta and its bright cheerful people, or the words we saw written in English on one of the school buildings: 'Gather courage, don't be a chicken-hearted fellow.'"

Tilman and company discovered frequently checked-out works of English literature in the library. So, after several hours of poking about, I locate a new library with selections of Hindi, Japanese, Nepalese, and English books—mostly detective stories and glitzy romances sandwiching a lone Shakespeare. But across town, I uncover a neglected reading room, where two men stink sweeter than gin, sleeping off last night's binge of potent rakshi. Strewn about a cabinet are a dozen works of literature, pages still uncreased and unthumbed. According to the frontispieces, Cowles and the Houstons donated these books in 1950.

As I make my way back to the bus, people stare. I am as much an anomaly to them as they are to me. The "gather courage" motto is long gone. Streets stink of urine, litter is heaped indiscriminately, houses are in need of a whitewash, a beggar pulls on my sleeve. Clearly it's paradise lost. Again, I'm disheartened—as Houston told me, "Roads have done more damage than any mountain tourism."

Tenje has vanished, so I bus the last miles to Hille alone. As I hang out the window to breathe fresh air, a deranged man pulls the window down onto my neck. After extricating myself, I shove him away, and he shuffles off to torment someone else.

The Himalayan Hotel in Hille is rocking with rakshi drinkers, but I am so overloaded with the dizzying kaleidoscopic bus rides, I fall asleep in the midst of arguments, a loud radio being switched from channel to channel, and clouds of cigarette smoke penetrating wafer walls. Sometime after midnight, a man pounds on my door, screaming with an alcohol-thickened tongue, but when I determine the hotel is not alight, I plunge back into deep and distant sleep. Like other nights, I have violent dreams, dreams of Chevrolets and cosmopolitan streets, and the ubiquitous dream of my American ladylove. When the rooster crows at dawn, I come awake understanding that Nepal's culture will elude me until the U.S. is gone from my subconscious, until I can dream like a Nepali.

Tenje reappears in the morning, so we find the trail and walk downhill all day. At dusk, we stop at a lodge on the banks of the Arun River. I jump into a backwater and wash away the trail dust, thinking of Houston, who fished the river daily for the elusive Mah-seer, but came away empty handed. Back at the lodge, with a stroke of luck, two boys sell us a freshly netted Mah-seer. We dine on curried fish—Asian style—bones and all.

Oranges, corn, millet, rice, guavas, bananas, and grapefruit are grown all about this cornucopian valley, one of the deepest, longest river gorges in the world. Walking here verges on sensory overload, for it is at once jungle, farm, riverine, and a hive of human activity.

Even the spiders are fat from the bounty, perched like small falcons in the branches, waiting for insects to fly into their webs. Most anywhere else in the world, this resource-laden watershed would be heavily developed and mechanized so its abundance could be further capitalized upon. But in lieu of roads and truck transport, only heavily laden men, women, and children fill the trails, just as they have done for hundreds of years.

Nor has the laid-back (and smart) Nepalese coefficient of work changed in the last 39 years. "No one would grudge a man stopping in his tracks to scratch his head or light a cigarette butt," Tilman wrote, "marching as they did in close companionable order in single file, every such halt had the effect of stopping everyone else. On a narrow track no one could pass and on a broad track no one wanted to. Nor were these successive checks, caused by the whim or the need of one man, confined to one's own little bunch. If the traffic was dense, several hundreds of coolies would come automatically, and not at all unwillingly, to rest because two friends a mile away had stopped to pass the time of day."

Pregnant women, dogs, and slim puppies crowd each and every hamlet. Typically, children within whipping length of a dog practice frequent abuse. The people, however, are terribly friendly, crowding around us and smiling. I eat a sweet grapefruit the size of a bowling ball and explain (with Tenje's halting translation) that Nepal is much smaller than America, but much more beautiful. The men squat, the women hang back deferentially, and children stand around with hands in mouths or fingering my ruby colored pack. The adults smile to cover their curiosity, while I pull my t-shirt on, concerned that I might insult them.

I walk to the river, shadowed by a bevy of children. There is no one to talk with, for Tenje and I can only trade language lessons, but among the children I am happier than I have been in days—trading smiles and laughter is the universal language of both children and adults in Nepal. In particular, they press their palms together and say, "Namaste" ("I greet the God within you"); they are delighted when I parrot their reply.

I pull my clothes off and dive into the azure river to cool off; the children giggle. It's glacial, and as Tilman wrote, "Bathing in the Arun is rather too sharp a tonic."

That night we reach the airstrip town of Tumlingtar. Almost 39 years to the day of my arrival here, prior to the airport's construction, Tilman had found an airplane flying overhead to be a "disagreeable event." Tilman, a guardian of "fair means" in mountains, was uneasy about the changes that ensuing expeditions might bring to Nepal; Houston, a doctor, argued that Western health care and schools would only improve Nepalese living conditions. Although schools were eventually built in most of the mountain villages, health care is strangely lacking both here and throughout Nepal, despite Tumlingtar's easy airstrip access, despite the staggering sums of foreign aid money pouring in from around the world.

At one of the lodges, I meet a Canadian physical therapist on her annual flyby from Kathmandu. For the next few days, scores of crippled Nepalese straggle in from miles around to receive what little care the therapist can provide. She has made untold sacrifices to help these people but feels inadequate because her Nepalese is limited. "Because of beliefs in shaman cures and the difficulty of travel and communication in the hills," she says, "I am only treating the tip of the iceberg."

When Tenje and I move down the trail, we step aside for an anxious-looking man coming into town. On his back is a son with malformed stick legs and fear painted wide and terrible in his eyes.

In Dingla, we stay at a tiny unadorned home with one of the wealthier families and learn more politics. The well-educated head of the household says, "I could be thrown in jail if I told you what I thought of the king." I press him nonetheless, and he tells us that their king is one of the richest men in the world, while his people remain the poorest—particularly here, where the benefits of mountain tourism don't match that of the Everest and Annapurna regions. Meanwhile, our host explains that many Nepalese worship the king as a religious descendent of Buddha, despite their hunger and insufficient medical care. (Two months later, violent demonstrations reinstated power to other political parties. In the meantime, like Ferdinand Marcos, the king continues to siphon foreign aid money into his own coffers.)

On November 22, Tenje and I climb out of the arid Arun Valley. Over the next week, we will plug up, down, and across three more river sheds toward Everest. Today however, we climb out of pine forests and alongside thickets of rhododendron, where monkeys cavort beside the sparkling Irkhua Khola. As we first enter the high country, potatoes become the staple crop, while rice is carried up from the lowlands. The potato was introduced to the region in 1850, imported from an English garden. More than a century before tourists, the potato allowed populations to surge around the otherwise rocky and infertile high mountain soils.

In Phedi, a potato village, we drop our packs at the Sherpa Hotel. Tenje is overjoyed because he can now converse in Sherpa tongue rather than Nepalese. He immediately sets to work on the local supply of rakshi, a potent moonshine of fermented rice and whatever else the local brew master throws into the distillery pot.

I meet a British journalist, fresh from the Burma war for a vacation in placid Nepal. In two short weeks, he has become embittered with the king's greed and what he perceives as the commercialism of the Sherpa people. "Don't trust them," he says, "but when you get to a Rai village, you'll see how self-sufficient the Sherpas used to be before tourism."

Then I meet the nubile, 21-year-old, almond-eyed Sherpani who lives at the lodge. She is the most striking woman I have seen in Nepal. Normally Nepalese women are quite shy. But this sober young woman's first question, passed through Tenje's translation, is different: "Is your sleeping bag big enough for the both of us?"

I wince, and through Tenje's somewhat stuttering reply, I ask, "What would your mother say if she heard that?"

"You must like young boys then?" she replies.

"I don't want to take advantage of you," I say. "I don't want to give you the wrong idea about Americans." Tenje takes an inordinate amount of sentences to convey this message to her, and I wonder if he's leaving out the "don'ts" and adding something that I can't own up to.

Her reply is plaintive: "Take me with you." Even the drunken Tenje stops leering.

"Goodnight," and I all but sprint to my sleeping bag—alone.

Her actions reveal desperation uncommon of Sherpas. Her willingness is to forsake everything in order to eat other than potatoes, to escape her labor in the fields and in front of the fire, to wear dozens of dresses instead of one. At the same time, I know many wealthy Americans who would gladly trade everything they own for the peace of mind that most Sherpas usually possess.

In the morning, a bleary-eyed Tenje suggests that we hire porters to carry our packs over Salpa Pass. Tenje has arranged a commission with the two dirty-faced monkeys with tumplines, standing straight and smiling for my inspection. I can't help but smile, too, for they are good boys, and ready to work like demons, but I am too far removed from my Victorian forebears to go pack-less while the hired help carries my share.

My contention is that Sherpas may have gained the wrong impression of tourists, and vice versa. As much as I want to help the local economy and generate some work, I have always carried my own pack in the mountains. Paying young boys to labor mightily for a few dollars, while the great white Sahib prances along unhindered, seems an arrogant and elite gesture. I have come to Nepal to encounter both the culture and the landscape as a Nepalese might, to eat their food, to sleep in the flimsiest of huts, to sweat behind laden coolies on high passes and share their acrid cigarettes. Perhaps I am just cheap, but when I part with my rupees, it will be for a service where my hosts will hold their heads high. Undoubtably the Sherpas will continue to serve and even die for their softer mountaineer brethren from the West, but not for me.

I am sad for Tenje, and still grappling with the veracity of my observations—it amazes me that all of my friends' tales and all of the literature I have read is so different from my own experience here. Tenje admires Tenzing Norgay, the "tiger of the snows" and first man atop Everest, but through no fault of his own, young Tenje is more "tiger of the teahouses." He has never climbed a mountain and his previous trips were shepherding and cooking for wealthy tourists on the Annapurna walking circuit.

Instead, I believe tourists need to start serving Sherpas tea. Tradition be damned, for the last two decades of trekking commercialism has transformed good Tenje, like many other Sherpas, into a servant boy.

In Phedi 39 years ago, even Tilman took exception to the usual praiseful prose about Sherpas and wrote, "They were in fact carrying nothing but their own kit and some souvenirs with which to astonish their stay-at-home cousins. . . ."

At Salpa Pass wet snow frosts the ground and wets the air as a boy offers me a radish—I trade him a chocolate bar. For half an hour, I photograph the stone Chorten (a religious memorial) from different angles and try to match Houston's old pictures. When Tenje arrives he is shivering, so I make him dress and eat. He promises to stay away from the rakshi.

Down in the Rai village of Gudel, among proud people who have inhabited the mountain valleys long before the Tibetan emigrations, we stop and eat lunch. A man and his son sew vests with hand-cranked sewing machines, a child looks through my camera,

I pay a woman to heat us some soup. Tilman had written: "At Gudel they would have no truck with us." Even Tenje seems a little awed by these taciturn people, with their lack of tourist lodges, their society's absence of beggars, and their disinterest in selling me anything. But I admire their self-sufficiency.

From here we descend 2,000 feet to the river, then up another 1,500 feet to the village of Bung—presumably a daunting passage to the 50-year-old, travel-weary Tilman. Many Nepal trekking aficionados know his poem of the passage:

> For dreadfulness nought can excel,
> The prospect of Bung from Gudel;
> And words die away on the tongue
> When we look back at Gudel from Bung.

However, there is now an experience at least as memorable as the crossing from Gudel to Bung (with apologies to Tilman):

> In Bung today there is an abode extraordinaire,
> Lacking roof and on one's bottom also open to air;
> When duty calls tourists to this stone stall
> The pig stands waiting for presents to fall.

In Bung, we stay in a manicured lodge (the usual nine rupees per night) and are warned by an Australian couple about the trekking groups whom we'll see on the trail to Everest basecamp. I'm told that they treat villagers like serfs, insulate themselves from the culture by eating their own food, and generally overlook the essence of Nepal. In several days, we'll intersect the more popular tourist-laden trail, but for centuries of Nepal hill culture, these trails have remained a means of commerce and commute rather than a playground for tourists. Tonight I am happy to be one of only several Westerners amongst several hundred villagers.

Thirty-nine years ago in Bung, Houston and Tilman drank rakshi and bought a goat for 12 rupees; upon inquiry, I find that a goat will cost me 500 rupees—the inflation for tourists in Nepal approximates 20 years worth of car prices in the U.S. And instead of poisoning myself with anymore rakshi, I settle for a 100 rupees ($3.50 US) Star beer—reminiscent of a Coors, but brewed in Nepal and manhauled from Jiri.

The next day we labor up to the 10,000-foot Shipki La. During the 3,000-foot climb, we encounter villagers carrying baskets of firewood, or dragging fresh-cut, ten-foot bamboo poles. Since the Sherpa people started migrating into Nepal from Tibet 500 years ago, roughly half of the forests have been removed for farming, pasture clearing, and cooking fuel. Yaks, cattle, and sheep further graze the deforested slopes and prevent tree seedlings from taking. Although many foresters contend that the deforestation causes severe flooding in the southern plains, several learned scientists have proposed that agricultural terracing stabilizes the land.

Clearly the recent boom in trekking has increased deforestation. Virtually all of the lodges cook with firewood, so continued trekking shrinks the forests—already stunted by hundreds of years of agricultural demands. Furthermore, cooking with gas or electricity is difficult in many of the remote villages, although recently, conscientious trekkers have begun carrying their own fuel and avoiding firewood-heated showers.

In 1950, neither Sherpa nor Sahib foresaw the escalating deforestation or the soon-to-come hordes of trekkers and mountaineers. "He had a passion for building immense camp fires," Tilman wrote of one of their Sherpas, "nothing less than a holocaust satisfied him. Long before daybreak one would imagine that the sun had risen untimely, but it was only Danu rekindling the overnight bonfire."

Today, numerous foreign reforestation programs have implemented nurseries and re-seeding plots. The Ministry of Tourism will soon protect the Makalu area (behind us) with a National Park, while in front of us, Sagarmartha National Park (surrounding Everest) prohibits felling trees and shooting animals. High country Sherpas despise the Nepalese rangers (from the flatlands) who fine the firewood cutters and poachers.

Tenje, like most Sherpas, sees the problem simply. His people—whether guides, lodge owners, or merchants—profit from mountain tourists sitting in front of their fires, a far preferable alternative to poverty. But asking Tenje how he feels about the problem is akin to insulting Daniel Boone about clearing the forests in Tennessee 150 years ago. Ultimately, as a "wealthy," well-fed American, it is easy to criticize Nepalese environmental practices, until one recalls the vanishing Redwoods, or the clearcutting of northern New England 100 years ago, or the crew cut that Alaskan timber is getting today.

Just above the village of Karte, we surprise the Danphe pheasant (*Lophophorus impejanus*), Nepal's national bird. This bird of nine different colors pecks the soil for grubs just above us, standing out like a metallic blue-green flag in the undergrowth.

Tenje picks up a rock in hopes of procuring dinner, but fortunately, his former food-gathering genes have been supplanted by more entrepreneurial instincts; the rock falls short and the pheasant flashes off with a lustrous whir of bronze wings. In the 1950s, hundreds of these birds clustered the mountain villages; today's pheasant is the only one I will see for weeks. Presumably, farmers have wreaked a savage toll because the pheasants are often found eating crops. Other indigenous wildlife such as the musk deer (prized for its scent gland) and the snow leopard (fetching a high price for its fur) are now nearly extinct.

When we reach Lukla, I give Tenje an extra week's pay and the bus fare back home to Kathmandu. I loan him a sleeping bag, pack, sunglasses, mat, and headlamp, then thank him for his efforts. We arrange to meet at a hotel in Kathmandu, but he will never show. Although the Sherpas are inherently trustworthy and honest, young Tenje is only trying to get ahead, to stake his claim to the abundance of Western wealth.

Otherwise, Lukla is a nightmare. The airport town is its own subculture, so distinctly removed from the rest of Nepal's tranquil mountain villages that I fall into unexpected culture shock. Florid Germans, affluent Americans, camera-clad Japanese, colorful French, reticent Israelis, and spike-haired Brits crowd the airport terminal waving tickets, cursing unflappable Sherpas, and demanding immediate flights. This is not Nepal. I leave saddened.

As I climb closer to the biggest mountains on the planet, my envy for Tilman's and Houston's privilege only grows. "My humble Mecca," Tilman wrote of Namche Bazaar. "As we rode in I shared in imagination a little of the satisfaction of Burton, or of Manning when he reached Lhasa." Although it is still a paradisal village, the 30 houses of the earlier era have quadrupled and are now lit with electricity from a hydroelectric plant built in 1983. Although Namche was unvisited by Westerners prior to 1950, tourists now fill the town, where any single size, quality, or quantity of Western mountaineering gear or food can be obtained.

Higher still, I visit the remains of the Tengboche monastery, surrounded by tourist lodges. "The monastery possesses a library of 500 wood-bound books each in its own curtained pigeon-hole," Tilman wrote. "Among its rich furnishings are a gilt, life-size image of the late abbot of Rongbuk monastery and some very beautiful religious paintings . . ." Yet in 1988, the newly installed electricity started a fire that burned the monastery to the ground—rendering books and precious artifacts ashes. And tourists now only harass today's monks, whose fathers greeted the first Westerners with snorters of rakshi and great feasts. They shout, "No pictures!" when I lift my camera toward them on the trail.

Onward then. With winter coming, the night temperatures drop below zero, although it is quite warm in the sun during the day. The tourists are flocking out of the mountains like a great migration. One rotund trekker asks me where I'm going, and when I reply "Everest basecamp," he warns, "It's cold up there."

"Good," I reply, "it'll keep the tourists away."

"You are a tourist."

As a mountaineer, I have always felt that I was shunning the tourist haunts and paying homage to mountains while shivering on their sides, cupping my hands and drinking deeply from glacial streams. Here in the crowded Khumbu however, it comes as a revelation that I am just another one amongst hundreds of mountaineers who will subtly impact both culture and environment. Yes, I am a tourist.

Although I am warned by a guide from a trekking agency not to "poach peaks" without paying the Ministry of Tourism's peak fee, I have no intention of following his advice. His trips are rife with cashy clients who are probably searching for the same Nepalese culture that I am. These Westerners will spend several days on a one-day climb, moving like cattle amidst their own insulated subculture that will never truly interact with the Nepalese. Also, a peak fee would only buy me an unwanted sirdar and porters, and of course, provide further percentage to the despotic king. Furthermore, I have long believed that propriety can't be attached to mountains—certainly the Nepalese have every right to the mountains I love in North America. So I will poach my peaks from the rich, leave no trace of my passage, then give my money to the lodges, and let the Sherpa people benefit directly from my presence.

For now however, I am happy to trace Tilman's footsteps. Just above Pheriche, at 14,000 feet, Tilman waxed grandiloquent around their bonfire. He talked for hours. Alone with Houston, inspired by the most sublime of all mountains, Tilman's normally reticent tongue wagged with stories shared with few men on earth. He was the eminent explorer of his days, but today, he would avoid Pheriche, surrounded by tourist lodges, trampled hard by the madding crowds, burned dry of the juniper formerly encircling the village.

Outside the Ama Dablam lodge, the lodge owner snatches a piece of pink toilet paper blowing by in the breeze. "Paper, paper, paper," she says. "There is paper everywhere." Although Tsing Puti is self-composed like most Sherpa people, on a deeper level she is troubled because both her culture and landscape have been violated. Nonetheless, Sherpas may well be the most adaptable culture on earth; she carries the toilet paper inside to start her cooking fire.

Her floor is sod, her menu order pad is the backside of an Everest expedition's medical chart. Thirty-six years ago, Tsing Puti portered for Lord Hunt's Everest expedition. She is excited about tonight's party at the American-funded medical clinic, and shouts, "Part animal, part animal!" until the trekker at my side teaches her how to pronounce "party."

The volunteer doctors and nurses put on a great do. They have become an important cog in the community, treating both foreign trekkers and providing low-cost medical care for the Sherpas. When the trekking season closes, however, they will close the clinic until foreigners arrive in the spring.

A Sherpa with the t-shirt "Pheriche Beach Club" refills my glass with chang, the Nepalese equivalent of beer, teeming with bacteria, leftover bread, human saliva, or millet seeds.

Meanwhile, two raucous Brits drink Nepalese vodka, wisely abstaining from the chang. They outline their plans to enter mountaineering fame and sponsorship by climbing a nearby peak that Tilman and Houston (who made the difficult first ascent of Nanda Devi in 1936) would never have considered because of its intrinsic technical difficulties. In fact, Houston had written of the nearby Ama Dablam, "We could see no feasible route up this mountain." Times have changed.

Next morning, I stumble about in the dark, still bloated from the innumerable toasts of chang. I strap on a fanny pack and jog toward Kala Pattar, the 18,000-foot vantage point from which Houston and Tilman considered climbing Mount Everest. There is a raw pre-dawn wind—I stop frequently to warm my gloved hands. I pass countless piles of human feces bedecked with toilet paper, a train of firewood-laden Yaks, and trash dotting the earth as frequently as stones. On one hillside, dozens of Chorten cairns commemorate the Nepalese climbers killed on Everest since 1953.

In Loubouche, the sun comes out and the temperature rises 70 degrees. I pass more tourists. We are all on a pilgrimage to Kala Pattar, all vying to see the biggest mountain in the world.

I pass people sweating in immense down parkas, virtually hand held by their Sherpas—while I imagine my own impatience at such a task, I can see only compassion written on the guides' faces. Just below the top, a man shouts directions to me, mistaking me for one of his clients, as if I, like the rest of his herd, might stray from the well-worn trail.

I have deliberately abstained from the view until now. For just a moment, I block out the crowd around me, look up, then imagine the way Houston and Tilman saw this snow-covered black beauty before I was born. The Western Cwm is truly a surprise passage, hidden from view until 300 feet below me. A convoluted cascade of broken ice and crumbling glacier towers all but audibly roars down the mountain. Now I understand my predecessors' disinterest. There is nothing aesthetic, let alone safe, about the route in front of me. Surely it is the easiest way up the highest mountain in the world, but Tilman and Houston were driven to quality rather than quantity.

"This does not seem a reasonable route by which to climb Everest," Houston wrote. Several years later, Houston nearly summited on a much more difficult (albeit safer) route on K2. He believed in safety and the fellowship of the rope, so the numbers of

Sherpas lost in the dangerous Khumbu icefall over the years would disturb him as surely as war.

Tilman wrote, "I suffer increasingly from mountaineer's foot—reluctance to put one in front of the other." He also sensed that exploratory mountaineering was becoming a lost art in a mostly explored world, so he turned to sailing. Between the lines of his book *Nepal Himalaya*, Tilman clamored for the cultural experience, for the opportunity to travel where no other Westerners had. He would never return because he had tasted the purity of Nepalese culture untainted by outsiders.

I come out of my reverie and see that the crowd around me is growing. A fellow tourist asks me to take a picture of her, so I oblige, then sprint back to Pheriche.

The lodges are closing now. As I leave, so do the doctors. Soon, for a few short months between trekking seasons, Pheriche will be almost like before, despite widened trails and uprooted junipers. I wonder if the earth really does abide? Closed to tourists and left to the locals, would the forests grow back and the summits become sacred again?

Nonetheless, I climb Island Peak in a quick and joyful day (meeting a guided party on my way back down who will spend several days sieging the mountain), then become sick with the "Khumbu cough." This bacterial presence, the bane of teahouse travel, seems lodged in my lungs. So I avoid the lodges and cook my own rice while bivouacking beneath the stars. Late one night coming down from another peak, I become lonely, so I knock on a Sherpa family's door. The woman fixes me tea, and I bounce her child on my knee. I stutter the few Sherpa words I know to the husband, but this night the language barrier is broken by everyone's smiles. Other nights, I sleep in abandoned huts and drink from pure mountain streams and sing to myself as I cross high passes.

One of my final nights out in the mountains, I fall asleep in a yak pasture, surrounded by dung piles, the cowbells giving voice to the stars above. I dream that I am a Sherpa dressed in Patagonia-labeled clothes and expensive mountaineering glasses, walking in front of a large group of clients. There are yaks behind us, bearing great tables and chairs and silverware and china. Suddenly, a drunken yak herder trips over me, flashing her torch inches from my face; I wake up and shout "No!" then realize that the woman is also very startled.

A long moment passes as we stare into one another's faces, struggling to find the prerequisite form and dignity that is Nepal. My smile alone would be meaningless, and neither of us speaks more than a few words in one another's language. So as I steeple my hands she smiles and together we incant: "Namaste."

Tyson Spring Cave

John Ackerman

Editors' note: John Ackerman grew up in Burnsville, Minnesota, and began exploring the extensive labyrinth of mines under St. Paul as a boy. Today he is one of Minnesota's most accomplished cavers and has discovered dozens of miles of heretofore unexplored caves across the state. Since the late 1980s he has been a cave preservationist and, where possible, has bought the subterranean rights to caves from Minnesota farmers. In 2013 the New York Times *noted that Ackerman "is the largest private cave owner in Minnesota and might be the largest in the country, but nobody is certain because not all of his caves have been fully explored to determine their extent." He allows school groups and researchers access to his caves. Here he describes the exploration of Tyson Spring Cave, which his organization, Minnesota Cave Preserve, owns. In 2008 Tyson Spring Cave explorers unearthed the Ice Age antlers of a stag moose and, two months later, a saber-toothed cat skull, making the cave one of the most significant paleontological sites in the Upper Midwest.*

The gaping mouth of this cave system lies directly below a cluster of towering limestone bluffs in Fillmore County. And out of its inky black mouth flows a tempestuous vibrant volume of water, which cascades down large stair stepping blocks of rock, beginning its journey through the descending forested valley.

When I first laid eyes on this resurgence I was smitten, as I know previous generations must have been, dating back to the arrival of the Native Indians. Because the setting is almost utopian, no doubt our ancestors chose to make arduous journeys through the wild terrain in order to spend quality time there. But due to its remote site, historical information is in short supply. We do know, however, that shortly after the War of 1812 the United States government gifted approximately 120 acres to a war widow, who then deeded the property to Mr. Harper Tyson in 1862. He was obviously very proud of his cave, and sometime between 1875–1885 a professional photographer, who utilized the stunning new stereoscopic method, photographed the idyllic cave resurgence. Another historical photograph, taken by a succeeding landowner, can be found in the Fillmore County Historical archives.

It has been reported that the resurgence was a favorite picnic setting back then and that folks could venture into the 800-foot long cave using wooden boats. Unfortunately these early adventurers were prevented from penetrating deeper into the cave because the main passage ultimately became totally submerged in water. How frustrating this must have been, because during low water conditions it is almost certain that they could clearly hear a vivacious turbulent waterfall through tiny air gaps along the ceiling.

It wasn't until the advent of wetsuits that explorers could finally wade through the bone chilling water to inspect every foot of this cave in hopes of finding a route around the water filled passage. During the 1960s and '70s Ron Spong, founder of the Minnesota Spelological Survey, made multiple attempts to breath dive and snorkel through the water filled passage but was unsuccessful. During the 1980s a well known local caver, Roger Kehret, focused on the idea that if the talus pile of rocks just outside the entrance could be removed it may lower the water level inside the cave by several inches. He theorized that several inches of water was all that stood between himself and the continuation of the cave.

In 1985, while Roger was still actively pursuing his goal, MSS members Larry Laine and Steve Porter successfully dove through the sump using SCUBA gear. They returned with the good news that the cave indeed continued deeper into the unknown. Due to dangerous water conditions and the need to modify their diving gear, the second penetration into the new section did not occur until the following year. A third trip was made in May 1987.

In the meantime Roger was like a locomotive train, making deliberate and steady forward progress in his attempt to lower the water level so that non-divers could explore the cave. His efforts paid off and by now the water level had been lowered enough so that the tiny air gaps along the ceiling allowed safe passage deeper into the cave. Just after passing through this dangerous area the fabled waterfall was encountered, but soon thereafter the passage became totally water filled. On September 6, 1987, Roger summoned Dave Gerboth and myself to the cave for what he felt was the final hurdle in lowering the water level. Roger was confident that if a few inches of rock were broken away from a constriction near the waterfall that the result may be a slightly lower water level.

The three of us transported a sledgehammer and large chisel to the site, and after three hours we managed to chip a few inches off the top edge of the constriction. By now my knuckles were beaten and bloody, and because the water was so cold my hands were almost numb. When we turned around to inspect the water filled passage we were elated to see that a small "V"-shaped air gap had opened along the edge of one wall. We were all speechless as we felt and heard a torrent of air screaming through the newly created space, beckoning from beyond. I managed to tilt my nose into this tiny cavity and worked my way slowly ahead, into blackness. Eventually the air space grew and I found myself standing in a large spacious passage—the third person to do so, and the first person to enter this new cave system without SCUBA gear.

Soon Dave and Roger successfully worked their way through the slot without extinguishing their carbide lamps and together we began to move deeper into the cave. Unfortunately Roger had bloodied his nose and had broken his glasses during his foray through the slot passage and as a result decided to retreat with Dave. Without any consideration for safety I went on alone. I seemed to be drawn deeper into the cave like a magnet. This place was alive and vibrant. The turquoise blue water ebbed and flowed over numerous calcite dams and collected here and there into deep cavities, some of which required me to swim across. The further into the cave I traveled the more astounded I became. The main passage became wider and taller, and as I crested a bus sized limestone block I found myself standing in a huge room with a sandy floor. After catching my breath momentarily I rejoined the main stream passage, where the formations grew in size and color. After traveling one mile through this labyrinth I was totally awestruck.

Eventually I came upon another sump but could see several inches of air space and so I decided to risk it once again. This almost proved to be a fatal error on my part because I actually became lost in this passage with my lips scraping against the ceiling. I meandered throughout the icy cold pitch-black passage, sniffing for a way out, any way out. My neck muscles were eventually so fatigued that they were almost unable to hold my lips to the ceiling. Finally I made the correct turn and popped out into the continuation of the huge cave passage. Hours later, after traveling almost two more miles through stupendous cave passages I turned around and made my long solo journey out. Along the way I was enthralled by the dynamics of the stream passage and understood my fate if it were to rain outside, causing the water to rise even one inch. Why I thought I could cheat death I will never know. Maybe it was because I understood that great discoveries involve great risk.

Three weeks later fellow MSS caver Jason Engelhardt, my employee Bob Vanderweit and Dave accompanied me into the cave to continue the exploration. The day wore on and the miles passed us as we traveled past the original place where the divers had turned around. Our legs were beginning to feel a bit like rubber. My mind, however, was in overdrive. My anticipation peaked as I rounded each bend and marveled at the sights and sounds that lay before me. By early evening the others were trailing behind, and as I rounded another bend in the passage I discovered the route ahead was blocked again by water. I had found the "end" of the cave, but nonetheless, my adrenaline level was still soaring and I felt like I was flying.

On the way out of the cave while the rest of the party took a break on a sandy bank, I trekked solo down a long narrow side branch. The first part of the passage was very friendly but eventually the ceiling hunkered down and I had to move forward by crawling on my hands and knees. After a few hundred feet the ceiling became lower yet and I was forced to slide ahead on my belly. Eventually my belly and my back were both pressed tightly between the floor and the ceiling, and every little cobblestone that I slid over dug into my chest. I could hear a thundering echo ahead and so I was mostly oblivious to the pain. After following this passage for over one quarter mile the ceiling finally rose up, and as I stood up I was dumbfounded at what my eyes were seeing. I had discovered an incredibly tall decorated dome, perhaps the tallest in Minnesota. As I reveled at this stupendous dome, with my neck cocked all the way back, I felt a sharp pain in my right rib cage. Intuitively, I reached down inside of my wetsuit and pulled out an off-white golf ball sized cobblestone! This little nugget must have made its way there as I was bulldozing along the passage. For some reason I thought of it as a well-earned prize, and so I stuffed it safely back inside my wetsuit and began the journey back. When I returned to my van that evening I placed my special prize in a nice little niche inside the dashboard console.

I had been the first human to reach the far depths of this cave system and the experience had been etched into my very being.

I was 33 years old when I made that epic trip into Tyson Spring Cave and it has remained seared into my consciousness ever since. To this day I still have that special beige cobblestone, which I have kept in each one of the nine vans I have owned since then. One recent sunny afternoon as I was parked on a St. Paul side street waiting for a customer to arrive, I casually removed that memorable cobblestone from the little niche below my dashboard. And as I rolled it around in the palm of my hand memories of the cave came back to me with startling lucidity. Then it dawned on me that it had actually been 19 whole years since I had been in Tyson Spring Cave. As unbelievable as it must seem to most people, including myself, I had tested my luck countless times throughout the years and actually lived to see my 52nd birthday. As I deliberately placed the cobblestone back in its special compartment I paused for a few moments and then made an unyielding pledge right there and then that revisiting Tyson's would be a top priority.

And so it would be.

Two weeks later I found myself standing at the mouth of the cave, and that very same morning I disappeared into it, on my way to retrace my original journey into this amazing cave system. Although I had a support team available, I chose once again to make a solo reconnaissance into this formidable tempestuous cave system.

As I navigated through the low air spaces, the labyrinth of swims, negotiated over and under immense dislodged blocks of limestone, and strolled amongst massive delicate formations, the awesome presence of this 3.5–5-mile-long cave revealed itself once again. Upon reaching the immense dry room, I paused momentarily, gazed from end to end, and continued my journey deeper into the cave. I felt strong, electrically charged, and honored to be a witness to such an incredible environment. As I resumed my excursion along the main gallery, the formations appeared to be even more abundant, pristine, and grandiose than I had remembered 19 years ago. As I rounded a gentle bend in the passage, I abruptly paused under a large shimmering transparent formation, and glancing down at the myriad of colorful cobblestones on the floor, one in particular caught the glimmer of my light. It was beige, and was about the size of a golf ball. As I embraced it in the palm of my hand, my eyes returned to the immaculate formation overhead, and right then and there I made a firm commitment to myself that this cave system would forever remain pristine.

Today I am so pleased to announce that Tyson Spring Cave will indeed be perpetually protected. The Minnesota Cave Preserve has purchased property over the cave system and has secured subsurface rights, which includes the natural stream entrance and four other outlying caves. A 115-foot deep access shaft has now been created into the magnificent Tyson Spring Cave system, which will allow safe entry to cavers and researchers. I would like to thank Dave Gerboth, Charles Graling, Ted Ford and many others who have helped make this historically significant project possible. My heartfelt appreciation goes out to Clay Kraus, who was instrumental in making this vision a reality.

The Chugach

Dean Cummings

Editors' note: Dean Cummings is one of the greats of Alaska skiing—not just for first descents and extreme lines, but for understanding snow and snow safety and sharing his knowledge. Cummings grew up in New Mexico and became involved in outdoor safety education in his early teens while working as a guide assistant for the Santa Fe Mountain Center. He later went on to become the captain of the US Freestyle Ski Team. From the mid-1980s through the '90s, he made hundreds of first descents and won the World Extreme Skiing Championships in 1995. A pioneer of Alaskan helicopter skiing, Cummings is the owner, operator, and head guide of H2O Guides. His experience and diligence in developing the highest standards in guiding and education allowed him to secure permits on the largest tract of heli-ski terrain in North America: the Chugach Range in Alaska.

Two decades of guiding in Alaska have given Cummings an intimate knowledge of the snowpack and mountains and, coupled with his vision and commitment to guiding, have led him to found several education programs for both guides and the general public, including the North America Outdoor Institute (NAOI). He authored and crafted the "Be Snow Smart" education program, which annually reaches twenty thousand people with practical, easy-to-implement recreation safety procedures. Here he recounts three of the most significant first descents in the Chugach: the Tusk, the West face of Meteorite, and Mount Francis.

The Chugach Range is just incredible. The range has one of the highest concentrations of interconnected peaks and glaciers in the world with Alaska's deepest annual snowpack. I was stunned when I first arrived in 1991 for the World Extremes in Valdez. After making several first descents in the range, I realized that we needed to develop protocols not just to ski these peaks but to stay alive. My protocols eventually morphed into the Steep Life Protocols.

I founded H2O Guides in 1995, the same year I won the World Extremes, and am proud that this is H2O Guides' 20th anniversary season of guiding people down these mountains and providing the experiences of a lifetime.

People always tell me that I'm lucky to ski these big peaks, but the reality is that in the last 24 years of guiding in the Chugach I've only had a handful of perfect opportunities to make the biggest, baddest first descents, including the West face of Meteorite Mountain, the Tusk from the summit proper, and Mount Francis from the summit proper.

THE TUSK

In 2010 I attempted a Tusk ascent and descent with local heli-snowboard guide Sunny Hamilton, wife of H2O guide Mike Hamilton.

We attempted to climb to the summit proper, but while I was leading out the climb Sunny got cold, and it was getting late. That was three strikes, so I aborted touching the summit.

But I was still hungry to descend the Tusk from the true summit, down the direct face.

So in April 2011 I got my window and was dropped off on the summit by helicopter with 400 feet of 11-millmeter rope for a rappel.

It took 16 attempts to get the rope to run clean, and I had to recoil the rope each time. I was concerned about getting the rope stuck in rock each time, which would have forced me to do a technical down climb doing a variation off the backside.

On the 17th toss, the rope ran clean, and I started the rappel. I was under constant threat of getting injured or knocked unconscious by falling rock, and I was very concerned about severing the rope on sharp rock or getting stuck. I was already on strike two at this point. Strike three would be a rescue situation.

I successfully rappelled to a safe zone to put my skis on, and began the descent on 60-degree unsupported slope through a 70-degree three-dimensional double fall line that protected the main face. It was technical and strenuous, and I almost overheated.

Once on the main face, the most important part was skiing the spine to allow my snow slough, or an avalanche, to part around me.

After descending the main spine, I cut skier's right onto the fluted face then dropped through double cliff bands, over a bergschrund, and finally out onto Tusk glacier.

West Face of Meteorite

During the filming of *Global Storming* with Matchstick, I did the first descent of the West face of Meteorite Mountain, which was named after it was struck in 1927 by a meteorite that sheered off literally millions of tons of rock.

The West face is highly exposed with over 1,000 feet of cliffs for the first half. The second half is a couloir that exits over a mandatory 120-foot cliff.

The descent began blind with a convex bowling ball that went from 50–60 degrees working left to right with only one big rock above the couloir for a safe zone.

After skiing the first 500 feet my slough turned into a Class 2 avalanche that flowed over the 1,000-foot cliff. As I skied safe zone to safe zone, I watched three more point slide releases.

The only way to ski the couloir was to ski 300–400 feet at a time then get into a safe zone, skiing a little bit and hiding, going a bit more then hiding, so not to get swept over the 120-foot cliff by point slide releases.

Once I got 400 feet above the cliff I ran out of safe zones, so I had to be quick to make it to the edge of the cliff. Then 100 feet above the cliff I had to negotiate white ice. I used my skis like crampons to make it past the ice. It was a one way ticket at that point. I side stepped up about 12 feet above the cliff then did a sliding sideways jet turn so I could redirect my angle for the landing.

In the air the wind started to get under my legs and began to push, trying to force me upside down. I was able to gyro my arm to keep upright.

On the landing I lost a ski and did three huge flips over the bergschrund.

Even with the triple tomahawk landing it felt successful because it was such a burly physical descent with massive exposure, multiple point release slides, and the white ice.

Mount Francis

Skiing Mount Francis from the true summit was a 20-year dream. This descent involved endless logistics, research, and mental challenges.

Mount Francis is one of most aesthetic, north-facing slopes in the world. It starts with a mandatory 80-foot cliff jump below a 70-degree fluted clamshell entry.

I've climbed it twice, and flew in with film companies, but it was never the right time until April 2012.

With my Steep Life mission to share protocols, I knew if the conditions aligned I would go for it.

On April 17 we flew in with the goal to document my descent from the summit proper. If everything checked out on the aerial survey and summit scout I would do it.

The key ingredient was making sure I could get a visual of the take off and landing zones. I climbed to the top of a chimney skier's right of the clamshell for a vantage point where I determined that even if I didn't make a perfect landing I could still pull off some friction moves to self arrest and not tumble over the 300-foot cliff below.

The entry was a classic convex clamshell—40 degrees tapering to 70 degrees on 70-foot-long flutes. The snow was Goldilocks: not too soft but soft enough for punching arm anchors into the snow like a snow picket.

I worked down one of the flutes, using arm anchors and my ski edges. Halfway through I punched through a curl that was like a frozen ocean wave, and it was almost enough to mess with my mind.

I readjusted and got myself in position for the jump. This was the crux. How do you unhook from 70 degrees, do a jump turn, and get your tips, hips and hands facing downhill all in one motion for an 80-foot drop?

On take off it felt like I reached terminal velocity instantly.

My right arm never made it fully around, and my hips were behind and to the right. Midair I wondered how bad this might go. I flipped, and I could see the Lowe River and Prince William Sound 6,000 feet below. Time slowed down; it was surreal.

On impact, I flipped, and my right ski came off. On the second flip I was looking for my ski in midair so I could grab it. I didn't want to lose any equipment.

I self arrested and when I came to a stop my ski was right in front of me.

Then the reward for that tenuous descent and cliff drop was the perfect powder run. It was too good to be true. I skied fast and made big GS turns down perfect deep powder to the escape route above the 300-foot cliff and into the exit couloir, which was an incredible descent down a 55-degree powder spine.

I skied cautiously above the bergschrund to avoid ice chunks, and once over the 'schrund I had to navigate some crevasses, then with the light fading I made time to the lower cirque to get retrieved by the heli.

Nobody has dared to ski these three particular routes again. I ski these big peaks and document them to get people's attention, inspire them, and share the Steep Life Protocols that allow people to implement better terrain management, stay safer, and take their skiing to another plane.

This is The Steep Life—the risks we take as humans who are committed to getting in touch with nature and ultimately the protocols that help keep us safe allowing us that sweet privilege. It's the privilege of living in the moment, filling your lungs with fresh air, feeling your heart pounding, blowing your mind with visuals, hearing the sounds of nature, getting after it, loving it, benefiting from it, and recognizing that we need to give back to it, protect it, and respect it.

Bandit Border
&
Noah Was Here

Christina Dodwell

Editors' note: Christina Dodwell is one of greatest women explorers and adventurers in history. She has journeyed across much of Africa, the Middle East, Siberia, China, and Papua New Guinea by horse, camel, elephant, canoe, and microlight (small plane). Her adventurous life began, more or less, in 1975 with a trip to Africa with a girlfriend and two male companions. The two men stole the women's jeep. Stranded, Dodwell and her friend acquired two wild horses. After a year of travels, her friend returned home, but Dodwell carried on for three years, traveling by horse, camel, and elephant. "When you're thrown in at the deep end you either sink or swim," she told British journalist Mick Sinclair in 1985, "but I found it was such a learning ground and I enjoy the learning. Everything changes once you lose a vehicle and you're down to your feet or the horses, which we had. You can see the country in a different way because you can't carry everything that you need.' You can't carry food supplies or much water so one becomes much more dependent on the land and the villages."

The following two excerpts—"Bandit Border" and "Noah Was Here"—are from a series of remarkable solo horse journeys in Iran and Turkey collected in her 1987 book A Traveller on Horseback in Eastern Turkey and Iran.

Bandit Border

After Keyif and I had a last bath in Lake Van, we were ready to leave. I collected him from his stable the next morning at 6 a.m., was grossly overcharged but I had expected it, and was content that he'd been well looked after; his girth was one notch fatter.

I was making for Ercek Lake to the north-east, crossing over a mountain divide between the two lakes. At noon I stopped by a stream bank where turquoise kingfishers were diving for their lunch. I rubbed Keyif with some anti-fly treatment I'd bought from a vet, though I doubted it would work since we were too outnumbered; even the vet had been pessimistic but suggested that the flies might feel ill after biting Keyif.

Our afternoon's route lay along a dirt road in a beautiful valley bordered by mountains whose rocky outcrops were pink-red, and at the valley's end I could see a massive natural gateway of vertical rock flanking an empty space of blue sky. To the west it was black and rainy, and the wind was pushing the rain clouds into my valley. There was just about time to outrun the storm, with luck, so I set Keyif into a canter, and felt the first raindrops splatter against my back.

We never quite got caught, always just ahead of the storm. Five storm clouds were converging, and I could see rain falling from all of them, but when I pulled out my plastic rain-sheet Keyif freaked out, rearing up in a panic; it would be impossible for me to wear the rain-sheet and ride, or lead him in it. So much for my rainproofing. Kurdish women in the fields were hastily finishing tacking sheaves of barley; their red clothes making them stand out against the ripe corn.

Passing through the natural rock gateway, Lake Ercek lay below ringed by beaches and cliffs. I turned left up over a headland under an ominously black sky, though there was sun beyond and rainbow. From the headland a chain of small islands and rocks ran into the lake. We went down for a drink but the water was salty and Keyif spat it out in disgust.

We wandered along the lakeside and over headlands and long beaches. It was evening and people were herding their cattle and horses home. Keyif neighed frantically at them all, he was obviously back in good form.

I spent the night in the lakeshore village of Golalan, at the muhtar's cottage. A kindly man, he told me he had been muhtar here for fifteen years, the village didn't bother to hold elections any longer. In various cottages I noticed tapestries and pictures of a legendary creature which the villagers said used to live in the lake. The creature had a man's head with elaborate head-dress on the scaly body of a fish, like a merman except that its tail ended as the head of a serpent. The shape was curled around so that the serpent's forked tongue stuck out toward the man's head. The villagers said the creature's name was Sha Maral, it no longer lives in the lake, nor are there any fish.

We left Ercek Lake on a cart track up the mountains, but I lost the track. The valley led east and I was worried about straying too near the Iranian border. When we passed some cowherds they followed me and kept calling me back. I ignored them since the valley had now swerved north but when I stopped for Keyif to graze, one cowherd caught up and told me that my route would lead into a very bad area. He made throat-slitting gestures to illustrate his meaning.

He took me back to their camp, introduced himself as Ahmet, we drank hot water, since he had no tea, and he invited me on a treasure hunt. Later, at Ahmet's village, I met his brothers. They talked of Urartian gold crowns like the ones I'd seen in the museum at Van and they were convinced I must know something—or else why should I be there? I disappointed them by not having a treasure map to contribute to the enterprise but they decided I'd bring them luck anyway. One of the brothers drew a picture of circles and tree shapes which he said was the key to understanding the site.

I couldn't make head nor tail of their map but was willing to join the adventure. But when it transpired that we would have to go at night, I said no, how could I understand anything in the dark, I'd only trip over rocks. So we agreed to go at dawn. The secrecy was because they thought all the villagers would follow them and take away their prize.

Of the three brothers, Ahmet had the lowest status, no one gave up his cushions to him, or moved up to make room for him. He sat on the plain carpet, and after lunch he cleared away the tray which is usually the work of women. In this village I was treated as a man. I noticed that the women had enormously fat bottoms, wearing numerous wrappings under their skirts, which looked just like bustles. A couple of men here had two wives, one had three, and another had the Moslem maximum of four.

Very early the next morning I went with the brothers to where they thought the Urartian town had been, and they took me to a large rock whose face bore the very ancient inscription which they had drawn on paper for me the day before.

Although much eroded it was easier to understand on the rock than on paper. The circle enclosed a series of ornate crosses, not trees, similar to the Christian pilgrim crosses I had seen on the stonework of Aghtamar's island church in Lake Van. So I explained that I thought the symbols marked a holy grave or tomb.

The brothers had already dug a large hole at the foot of the rock, uncovering the masonry of old walls, and although they dug to shoulder-depth, we found nothing of significance. They decided to abandon that hole, which suited me since I'm not keen on tomb-robbing.

As we parted they gave me a list of villages I should pass through to reach Muradiye, since there was no direct route and they were worried about my safety.

I crossed a forbidding chasm and climbed its opposite side, up into mountains, through the first village on the list and again up a long steep zigzagging climb. From the top I could see both lakes, Lake Ercek behind us and the northern tip of Lake Van ahead.

The track descended and looked as if it were headed down to Lake Van. That didn't suit me so we took off across country along the mountain contour, and by midday had reached an alpine plateau, endlessly rolling and rich with pasture. There were small yailas, pink landslides of rock, many fresh springs, streams and turtles. The cool breeze made it a glorious day. We entered a hidden plain extending about ten kilometres, Keyif cantered along in top form, he simply wasn't interested in walking, and his excitement added to my sense of exhilaration. It was a memorably wonderful ride.

I stopped four times to let Keyif eat, roll and relax, and midafternoon we paused at a hamlet so I could have lunch, but rather regretted it because of silly young men and no stable for Keyif who got left in the sun and wouldn't touch the thistle-full hay that the villagers gave him. The silliness of the youths was mostly because they too were convinced I'd got a treasure map—it's odd how people were obsessed with treasure hunting, and they wanted me to give them my gun, which I don't have, and didn't I know any karate or self defence, which made me think they were planning to rob me. Also I had a tick inside my trouser leg which I couldn't get at to kill.

So I left after half an hour, keeping a sharp watch-out behind me for followers, and we sped over the hills. Still going north, down through a boulder field and sloping mountain spur; gently down, the major descent would come later. I hadn't realised how high we had gone.

A movement attracted my eyes, the lumbering of a brown bear, fortunately moving away from us. I was told that they could be quarrelsome when coming out of hibernation. Later I spotted another hamlet and thought there should be a way down from it but the track proved to be an animal path which clung to the side of a ravine. At times I felt sure I had mislaid the right way and was only on a goat path. This was probably true, since by halfway down the slopes became perilous, and the path narrowed along a sheer drop. I slipped dislodging some stones that fell vertically for fifteen metres. The inner side of the path had such prickly thistles that leaning inwards was impossible. In patches the path had eroded away leaving gaps that Keyif stepped over gingerly.

At one steep patch I slid down on my back, holding the reins to stop my fall. Keyif stood firm. Very testing for him, the worst I had asked of him so far, but he wasn't fazed by it. The steepness of the angles necessitated a crupper to stop my saddle and saddlebags sliding forward on to the horse's neck, and I suddenly realised that the tasselled woven strap which hung from the back of the saddle was not only decorative. I fitted it as a crupper and it worked well.

Crossing landslides and loose scree, I tended to go down toboggan-wise and wished that Keyif wouldn't keep taking a higher route. If he slipped I would be cushioning his fall!

The descent took three hours, and we came down into a valley beyond the north-east tip of Lake Van. I stopped at a village for tea, and let them persuade me to stay the night. The men here also asked me about treasure maps, and showed me some local rock-inscriptions of crosses, square W's and other squiggles. We had rice pudding running with butter for supper. The night was one of heat, mosquitoes, and bed bugs that put red weals on my stomach and legs.

In the morning as I rode out of the village, a dog the size of a Saint Bernard bounded up to attack. I drew up my knees and rattled Keyif's reins as if to tell him "Do something," and when the dog tried to bite Keyif's hind legs, the horse kicked back. But one got me later that day as I was walking along the road to Caldiran. A large Anatolian came bounding out of a shed snarling furiously. I did the worst possible thing, I ran, and felt its teeth snap into my leg. Pain and fear shot through me but luckily the dog let go and ran back into the shed. I limped away, wondering if not having a tetanus injection would be more harmful than a visit to the local hospital, if there was one.

I decided to look for anti-tetanus vaccine in Caldiran, the next town, which we reached at sunset. Someone yelled "Turist, gel, gel" (come here) so I went to ask where to find a water tap for the horse, and I stayed there, with Keyif in the empty cottage next door. My host killed a chicken for supper which we ate with melon and watermelon. It was a cold evening, I put on a sweater and at night was grateful for the thick quilt.

The hospital was not open at 8 a.m. so I went to the nurses' house. The nurses were delightful, though the dispensary was wait-ing for a new supply of anti-tetanus vaccine, due to arrive some day soon, but the girls assured me that the hospital at Dogubayazit should have some. And they gave me a little bag of sweets for the journey as a touching gesture of goodwill.

I rode north across a great flat plain where the battle of Caldi-ran had been fought in 1514, when the Ottoman Sultan Selim the Grim had decisively defeated the Persian army before forging on to conquer Syria and Palestine.

Our road led close to the Iranian border. A dirt road with parts still under construction, in a year's time it would be asphalted, but now it was perfect for a horse.

Lonely and desolate, we pattered through a vastness where black rock was eroded in turbulent seas of jagged teeth. A strong wind kept the day cool and emphasised the desolation. I paid attention to the slightest movement, being aware that there was a very real danger of bandits.

As the land unfolded I saw a distant crater of a large volcano to the west and realised that the jagged expanses of black rock were actually huge tongues of lava. The volcano's cone was topped with snow, and the patches between the black tongues were verdant green, a startling combination. Keyif danced along, giving me a top-quality ride.

We reached an army outpost, here to guard the frontier, and the sentry called me over to check my passport. He looked at the photograph, then at me, and queried "Bayan?" (woman?). Other soldiers came over and seemed equally puzzled so I took off my man's cap and let my long blonde hair show. This earned me an invitation into the office for a glass of tea under the regulation portrait of Atatürk. The soldiers were patriotic young men doing their eighteen months' national service on one of the remotest frontiers. They had no transport to go into town, their supplies being brought in by truck, so they never left their station except to make foot patrols in the mountains. They claimed they didn't mind the discipline and it occurred to me this was just as well. Without discipline, they might all have leapt on me like a roomful of Keyifs with one mare.

The soldiers said that martial law had ended this week in eastern Turkey. I hadn't known the region was in that state. They also said there would be three more military outposts along the road, and warned me that when I descended into the lowlands I would pass through a notoriously wild and lawless place called Kizil Ka where even they dare not stop, and their vehicles have frequently been stoned. Those people are the worst type of Kurd they told me, lawless and violent bandits. The commander added that there was no alternative route, I would have to ride through Kizil Ka, but I should keep my wits sharp.

At the second military outpost the soldiers were playing volleyball. My passport was checked and the news relayed that here was a girl, and when I explained that I'd ridden from Erzurum via Van they all began to applaud.

Later, passing through a windswept empty area, I looked for a hidden niche where Keyif and I could take an hour's undisturbed rest. The giant lava flow with its grassy inlets offered concealment, and some way back from the road I found a good space, unloaded the baggage, tethered Keyif and, suddenly, realised that we were not alone. Someone else was hiding here too. I could see his feet in worn leather boots sticking out from behind some rocks and, thank goodness, he was asleep.

My first instinct was to flee, but not without my horse and baggage. At that moment Keyif found the stranger and snorted, waking him. The man was startled, he scuttled backwards and hissed at Keyif. Then cautiously he poked his head out from behind the rocks. My heart was pounding, but it occurred to me that perhaps the man was just as frightened as I was. We stared at each other for a frozen moment. His was the unkempt face of a thin twenty-year-old who had not shaved for weeks. His expression was very wary. I couldn't think how to react, so in the end I waved my hand at him politely and greeted him in Turkish. His head poked out further and he replied not in Turkish, but Farsi.

He walked over and scrutinised me then asked "Do you speak English?" I nodded, my surprise left me speechless. He asked for food, saying he'd hardly eaten for a week, so I gave him my picnic lunch of bread, eggs and tomato. I meant for us to share the picnic but he ate so ravenously I let him finish it. Between mouthfuls he talked and I pieced together his story.

A fugitive, deserting from the Iranian army, he had walked for eight days through the Kurdistan mountains to seek asylum in Turkey. He had been afraid to walk by day because the Iranian army or Revolutionary Guards would have shot at him, mistaking him for a Kurd; and afraid to walk on moonlit nights because the Kurds would have shot him, mistaking him for a Revolutionary Guard.

He was well-educated and spoke English fluently, and explained his reason for deserting. "I was likely to die crossing those mountains, but I was sure to die if I stayed in Khomeini's army."

He bombarded me with questions, did I know where there was a collection point for other Iranian deserters? Actually yes, I did know because in Van I had met a group of them, most of whom had paid the Kurdish mountain-folk about $1500 each to bring them out on horseback. Even their stories had been grueling, riding by night in constant danger. So I told him the name of the place where he could find the others, and explained that as I understood it from them, UNESCO gives $500 for each man's food and lodging, but that he was not yet safe since Iran offers $1000 for every man sent back. After twenty days in Turkey he could apply for work, and would need to go to Istanbul to ask UNESCO for a passport. But it would not be easy and his Iranian money was almost worthless here in Turkey.

As Keyif and I approached the third military post I heard some shots from up ahead. Creeping forward and scanning the mountains, I noticed the movement of a man on a hill summit attracting the attention of a second man on another summit. It seemed reasonable to suppose they were soldiers on lookout duty. They didn't appear agitated, probably they were just firing to make sure their rifles worked.

There was no trouble and I cleared the checkpost without delay. They said it was twenty-five kilometres to Dogubayazit, the same distance as both other checkposts had told me! Beyond it the mountains became beautiful with thick meadow grasses and the black tents of nomadic yailas dotted across the undulating vastness. This was one of the most scenically glorious roads I had used so far.

We had not yet reached the notorious Kizil Ka; Kizil means red, so I stayed alert for some sign. The land to the west fell away in a series of parallel mountain ridges outlined against each other. Suddenly we came over a hilltop into a magnificent panorama with snow-covered Mount Ararat looming above the mountainous horizon.

Mount Ararat is unequalled in the world for the height it rises above its surroundings. Even Mount Everest at nearly 10,000 metres is only about 3,500 metres above the glaciers which define its base. Ararat's summit is 4,270 metres above the plain of Dogubayazit, although in total altitude the mountain is only 5,180 metres. Its height is made more impressive by its shape and solitary position, growing from a flat plain almost without foothills. Ararat was still far away yet already it seemed to fill the sky.

Closer to me, about one kilometre ahead, was a massive pyramidal triangle of red rock. This was the red sign I had been watching for. The village shortly after it would be Kizil Ka. I dismounted to collect a pocketful of stones (for retaliation), and decided to try going through the village on foot, which might look less aggressive. Though the dogs could be a problem, and I left my stirrups ready for quick mounting.

It was a fairly successful idea, but I could tell that Keyif was being peppered by small stones because he pranced along fast. I smiled and greeted the elder villagers, it was only the urchins and youths who threw stones. Once clear of the village I swung into the saddle and we galloped away. Stones rattled behind us but we were quickly out of range. However I was congratulating myself too soon.

A man on horseback galloped up behind us and, instead of passing, he slowed to keep pace with Keyif. This was potentially a bad sign. So I made polite conversation with him; admired his horse, told him about my journey, and my husband in the next town. Keyif was snorting and I warned the man that he would kick and strike if the other horse came too close. Keyif played the part well. At one point the man tried to make Keyif throw me, but I'd kept Keyif's mouth so soft that he was easy to bring under control.

When we reached a flock of sheep and three shepherd youths, the horseman said goodbye. I was relieved. But the shepherds blocked my path waving sticks and demanding money. I politely asked the horseman to tell them to let me through. He did try to help me, and chased off one of the shepherds but the others attacked me with sticks and stones. The road was so steep and rocky it was impossible to run, and the road sides were even rockier. Pure violence was written on the shepherds' faces. They knew they had me cornered. Keyif reared and plunged as the shepherds brandished their sticks and pelted us with hefty sized rocks. One hit my shoulder and another just missed my head.

We weren't going to get past without help so I commanded my ally on horseback to come over. He came and Keyif dodged behind his horse, passing the shepherds who then leapt at my saddlebags, tearing into them with their hands, but Keyif danced clear before they had managed to break anything. I remembered the stones in my pockets and began to hurl them at the youths. Their eyes went murderous, and they ran at me.

Clapping my heels to Keyif's sides we didn't quite manage to get away before they had grabbed the back pocket of one saddlebag and my reins. I kicked one youth in the ribs to make him let go, and Keyif responded to my gallop command. The youth at the back clung on for several paces before letting go. Keyif and I raced down the steep track.

Several times Keyif nearly fell, but the hail of rocks still hitting him and me deterred him from slowing down. We had escaped. Glancing at my saddlebags I saw that the shepherds had succeeded in stealing my water-flask, Keyif's tether, and a few other things. But we weren't going back.

It was sunset, I stopped at the next village and asked if there was a safe place where Keyif and I could stay the night, explaining that I'd just had a bad experience in Kizil Ka. The men were stroppy, looking at me with unfriendly eyes, no one would take the responsibility of housing me. They suggested I kept on riding.

"Nothing would make me ride in this hostile place at night," I retorted. "My horse is tired, we need shelter."

A boy was ordered to take me to a military camp beside the village, where I dismounted and shook hands with the apparently senior men before voicing my request. Not that I wanted to stay at their camp, just to make sure they would treat me with respect. The muhtar happened to be there and he said that I would be welcome to stay at his house, and my horse would be safe in his stable because his property was enclosed behind walls whose outer gate was locked at night.

During the evening he told me that he had been the muhtar for five years and he certainly didn't want to be elected for another term, the work was all forms of trouble. He and his family were delightful people, I wished I wasn't too worn out to enjoy the evening. The night was abysmal, the bedding full of fleas, I awoke every few minutes and eventually just sat waiting for morning to come. It seemed likely to me that it's only the bedding which is stored without regular use that has fleas. Extra quantities of bedding are a status symbol, but it can go unused for years. At breakfast the muhtar asked me if I had slept well, I didn't have the heart to tell him the truth.

Rather than take the road to Dogubayazit and Mount Ararat, still twenty-five kilometres away around a mountain barrier, I decided to try a shortcut over the mountains. The muhtar agreed that one of the ravines would take me the right way. After passing the fourth military checkpoint I turned east, it was easy to keep my bearings since Mount Ararat towered into the sky way above the nearer mountain horizon. At the end of the plain we began climbing into hills, using a dry riverbed. It steepened into a ravine, progress was possible on a sheep path, but it changed course and as we closed in under the mountains I lost sight of Ararat's peak. So we went by God and by guesswork. My saddlebags got torn by rocks along the inside of a narrow cliff ledge but I stuffed a plastic bag under the tear and it plugged the gap.

At the head of the ravine was a spring, Keyif and I both tried to drink from it but he muddied the pool. Above this was a hill crest, we hurried up it, I was impatient to see whether I had picked the right ravine. We went over the crest, but another bigger crest lay ahead. Then slowly I saw the summit of Ararat appearing above my ridge, growing taller with every few metres that I climbed. Cloudless snowy flanks, smooth sweeping cone stretching down towards earth level, it seemed to keep growing until I reached the crest and then it lay before me, straight ahead.

From my highland vantage point I could also see the town of Dogubayazit still a few hours away down on the plain, and the ancient palace of Isak Paşa, which I hoped to visit later.

Near me on a mountain shoulder a Kurdish shepherd was brewing tea. He called me over; for obvious reasons I wasn't feeling friendly toward Kurdish shepherds but my desire for a cup of tea overcame my reluctance. He had two hundred sheep and he showed me how he played his flute to them. Its notes were reedy and zingy and its song carried on the breeze among the sheep and over the hills. My faith in human nature began to flow back into me.

He also showed me his favourite sheep, a woolly ram whose corkscrew horns indicated his descent from wild moufflons. Some young shepherd boys sauntered over to say hello, and respectfully called me Agha, a man's title. I thought about the line between distrust and caution, and how I prefer to trust people than to expect the worst, believing that in general one has a choice over whether one brings out the good or the bad in people.

Time stood still, it was a scene which didn't seem to have changed since men wrote about shepherds in the Bible.

Filling the background was the mighty Ararat, a mountain revered as holy by Christians, Moslems and Jews. On impulse I asked the old man if he thought that Noah's Ark was on Mount Ararat, and his reply was an unhesitating yes. He said all the local people know it's there, though they haven't seen it.

Noah Was Here

The descent to the town was long but not difficult, we reached it at noon and I put Keyif in a public stable run by a half-wit.

My first chore was to go to the hospital and have an anti-tetanus injection against the dogbite. My leg didn't hurt any longer, in fact the skin had gone numb which was worrying but the bite was healing well. After the injection I stopped at a chemist for flea powder, then went to the army headquarters. My purpose here was to try and obtain a new water-flask from their stores, to replace the stolen one, since it was impossible to buy a proper metal flask in the town shops, and the cheap plastic bottles on offer would split with rough handling.

In explaining why I needed a replacement flask the soldiers misunderstood what I wanted and they took me to the gendarmerie who promised to try and get back my original flask. It seemed they were longing for an excuse to teach Kizil Ka a lesson. That was fine by me and I hoped they would succeed. They told me to report back the next morning.

As I walked down the road two young school-girls latched on to my hands. Laughing and skipping, they led me to their home and invited me to stay. They were learning English at school, so I gave them an hour's reading practice in the afternoon.

Later I walked out of town to visit Isak Paşa. The palace is visible from afar, perched in a dominating position among sharp escarpments of green rock; its walls, dome and minaret stood out in sunlight against a black, threatening sky. Built in the 1700s by a Kurdish chieftain, its style is a mixture of Seljuk, Ottoman, Georgian, Armenian and Iranian. The entrance is magnificent, even without the gold-plated doors which the Russians took away during their 1917 invasion. Inside the first courtyard ornate stonework is carved in the Iranian style of animals and flowers instead of Moslem geometric motifs. Beneath the mosque a marble stair-case leads to the graves of Isak Paşa and one of his wives. There is a warren of small interconnecting rooms and dead ends and since I was being followed by a young man I climbed on to the walls, and toured the palace from above.

The floor of the throne room is superbly tiled in black and white marble and it has carved stone pillars, while each small individual room of the harem and children's apartments has its own fireplace with an elegant half-conical mantel, chimney breast and windows. The sky behind the palace now glowed as late sun lit the black clouds.

Isak Paşa seemed deserted except for its caretaker and my Kurdish shadow. He came up to me as I left and said he was also walking back to Dogubayazit. Rain began falling, increasing in ferocity until hailstones were stingingly painful. We sheltered in a ruined building and although the man was most helpful about pointing out the various other ruins in the jumble of fallen masonry covering the mountainside, he was very tedious with his suggestions of how we could keep warm together. I said that if I didn't hurry back to Dogubayazit my large jealous husband would be angry; and despite the rain I opted to run down the mountain, taking off my sandals and using a short cut to meet the road at the bottom. The man ran with me, to show me the way, quite amicably still offering me his body every time I paused for breath. Apart from that the views were stunning and the short turf with its stubby red flowers and feathery plants underfoot made for lovely running.

The man finally gave up on me and soon afterwards I reached the road. Still three kilometres to go, and still pouring cold rain, so when a tractor and cart came along I accepted a lift. The four young men in the cab offered to let me drive and since the driver's seat was safer than being squashed in their midst, I drove. I hadn't driven a tractor before, the cart made it swing around and slow to accelerate, but with four men trying to grope me I put my foot flat on the pedal and hoped the load of sheep in the trailer wouldn't fall out.

The roadsides banked steeply and I couldn't see the potholes because the windshield was caked in mud. More mud came flying up from the wheels into the cab, but without mishap we reached the school-girls' house and I jumped out. They were just sitting down to supper, tablecloth on floor, the girls tucked the cloth into their shirt necks. What a sensible idea. And we all dipped into the communal bowls of meat stew, pasta, yoghurt, and salad, a delicious meal. Despite the humble appearance of the house, the family was obviously not poor. They had a television, video, fridge, and a servant girl who was an orphaned relative. Listening to the news on television I heard that there had been an earthquake a few nights previously in this region. Although I must have slept through it, the shock waves had stretched to Ankara.

In the morning when I went to feed Keyif I found that chickens had nested overnight in his manger. They hadn't allowed Keyif to eat his hay, and they had laid two eggs in it. I moved him into a private room, fed him and shut the door so the chickens could not tease him any more.

As arranged, I reported to the gendarmerie and was surprised and impressed to see my water-flask and horse ropes lying on the desk. I congratulated the men on their efficiency. The rest of the day was spent quietly writing letters and mending the tears in my saddlebags, until 6 p.m. when I went to give Keyif his evening feed. The stables were locked and the half-wit had gone home. I couldn't leave it at that because I wanted Keyif to gain weight, he needed to eat plenty, so I started looking for a way in.

The local children who had accompanied me to the stables said they could get in through the roof. We climbed on to the flat roof and found a series of small ventilation holes. I knew that one of them had a shallow drop to an empty loft beside Keyif's stall, and I managed to squeeze through it. The drop was head height, but it wasn't until I climbed down into Keyif's stall that I remembered that I had bolted his door against the chickens. His hay and barley were in the next room. So I tried to climb out, and couldn't make it. I got my arms out but could get no leverage to lift myself. Hopelessly stuck, the situation was so absurd that I began to laugh. It's silly what people assume they can do. Finally a boy climbed down and let me stand on his back to get out.

Then we did what I should have done in the first place, went to the house of the stable-keeper, and he unlocked the stables for me. In the meantime another horse had arrived to be stabled overnight. I brought Keyif out for water, he took one sniff at the other horse, a mare, and lunged at her.

I couldn't hold him and my feet slid through the wet dung on the floor. The mare was kicking at Keyif, I was pulling with all my might, the mare's owner was shouting, I got kicked by the mare and trodden on by Keyif as he leapt on to her back, trying to rape her. Fortunately he missed and I managed to wrap his tether around a pole and pulled him away.

The man quickly took his mare into another stall and I apologised, leading Keyif away in disgrace. Life was never dull.

Mount Ararat, I pondered which way to ride up it. We must assume that Noah was the first man to climb down Ararat. But the first to climb up it was a German called Dr. Parrot who made the ascent in 1829. The easy approach from Dogubayazit didn't appeal to me since today most climbing groups go that way and it sounded crowded. When you've got a whole mountain, why follow the beaten track?

A south-east route would have taken me up on to the col between the great and small Ararats, but this alpine pastureland would be full of Kurdish yailas, and I had been told stories of a couple of American climbers who had everything stolen, including their boots.

The north and east faces of Ararat look into Russia and the area is prohibited to tourists, a shame because from there one can see up the abyss, a 3,000-metre chasm that splits the mountainside up to its summit massif, and it is overhung by 1,000 metres of glaciers. So Keyif and I would try a western approach. Once there was a village called Ahora and a monastery dedicated to St James on the north side of the mountain but both were destroyed by the massive earthquake of 1840 which threw the Araxes river out of its bed in the plain below. Today a new village stands nearby, and the north side has the added curiosity of a rocky outcrop shaped like the prow of a ship, which has often been mistaken for the Ark.

I liked the idea of looking for Noah's Ark. Soon after the 1840 earthquake there had been various sightings of the Ark, the first by a team of Turkish surveyors and workmen who went to check for danger of avalanches. They reported finding the front section of a large boat protruding from a glacier. Experts were sent to examine it and they climbed into some of the boat's well-preserved storage holds, but complete examination was not possible since most of it was still enclosed in ice.

In 1893 the highly respected Archdeacon of Babylon and Jerusalem, Dr. Nouri, launched an expedition. He too found the Ark and announced that he had entered the bows and stern, although the central part was still icebound. He mentioned very thick hull timbers held together by 300-centimetre pegs. The archdeacon was an intelligent and educated man, speaking over ten languages, and a friend of the American President Roosevelt, and it seemed unlikely that his story was a hoax.

Other reports came from Russian pilots during the First World War; stories that were initially laughed at then checked out by senior officers, who agreed it was true, the Ark was still there. The Tsar authorised an army expedition. It returned with photographs, but these were lost during the Russian Revolution.

In the Second World War another Russian expedition claimed to have located the Ark, badly rotted by this time and in the process of submerging back into a glacier.

While I was riding through Turkey, an American had been applying for permission to dig for Noah's Ark. He believed he knew where it now lay and was coming armed with special electronic equipment. But at the last minute the Turkish authorities had rescinded his permit and decided to investigate his spot for themselves. I felt a little sorry for him. Personally I didn't expect to find the Ark, but that didn't stop me from looking.

The next morning dawned clear, and Keyif and I set out via the corn-merchant, where I strapped some extra barley in a sack behind the saddle, and saluted the gendarmes who had recovered my stolen goods. It took only ten minutes to leave town, Keyif was so fresh he raced along skittishly and shied at every vehicle on the road.

Once clear of the town we headed towards the west side of the mountain, aiming to run up between two parallel arms of lava. Before long the land underfoot became spongy and I could see reedbeds and marshland ahead so we detoured to the west and tried again. The morning sun was building up a hellish heat, yet high above were glaciers.

The slopes were extremely tricky, the giant lava flows were jagged with crevasses that Keyif could not cross, the land between lava tongues was boggy, much wetter than would be expected after rainfall, and it made me agree with the recent scientific theory that Mount Ararat contains a vast lake inside its bulk. People had warned me that water is a curious problem on Ararat because although there is a massive ice-cap there are very few springs or streams. And their length is short, they flow back into holes in the mountainside. A vast subterranean cavern is plausible when one considers the inner working of molten volcanic activity, and it ties in with the last eruption producing steam and gases instead of lava.

Reaching an area where the marsh had dried to a crazy-paving of crusty slabs I heaved a sigh of relief. Keyif was less sure, he didn't like the fissures between them and he was not at all keen to walk where I directed him. At first the crust supported his weight and we progressed quite far until suddenly it gave way.

The slabs cracked and dust exploded upwards. Keyif floundered, thrashing with his legs but was unable to find any firm foothold, and we were sinking fast. I was almost blinded with dust and shock; realising the dry bog was probably made of volcanic ash, possibly bottomless.

We had already sunk down over one metre, but Keyif had managed instinctively to turn around and was plunging desperately towards the point where we had entered. All I could do was cling on to his mane and shout encouragement.

That was the first of many dry and wet quagmires that we fell into over the next twenty-four hours while Mount Ararat lived up to its popular reputation as a mountain that does not wish to be climbed. Ancient nomads believed it was guarded by angels and forbidden to men. A lot of talk nowadays centres on its dangers, like the zone of snakes. But I would see for myself.

Keyif and I were battling into a strong headwind and I could feel rain drops coming from behind us. With luck the wind would push the rain away. We reached about 3,000 metres; I wondered how long it would be before Keyif began feeling the effects of the altitude.

This western side, even down on the plain, is almost uninhabited and uncultivated, there seems to be no water. Above us tall rocks reached up like spires. The eastern plain is more populated, with villages that bear names such as Nakhitchevan, meaning "the place where Noah disembarked," and there is a site called Noah's burial place, and Ahora which means "vine plantation." Among the birds and beasts saved by the Ark, Noah also brought a collection of plants, and the vine was one of them.

The book of Genesis (chapter 9, verse 20) tells that Noah planted a vine after landing on Ararat. His son, Shem, took vines with him to the southeast and southwest. In fact, this geographical region is said to be the original home of the vine and, as I'd seen near Lake Van, it was an early centre for vine cultivation with sophisticated techniques of wine-making by 800 BC.

Despite the headwind, rain was now lashing down. As before, Keyif panicked at the crackle of my rainproof sheet and I had to fold it away. There was no point in seeking shelter since we were already soaked. I had noticed some yailas, but Keyif had spotted their horses and he began stamping and whinnying. That mare in Dogubayazit had scrambled his brains. Even the faintest horse-like shape in the distance made him prance with excitement.

The rain eased to drizzle and finally to wet mist. When I opened my saddlebags to put on dry clothes I discovered that rain had funnelled in through a hole in the plastic lining and everything was damp. The two most vital items were my sleeping bag, now useless, and my notebook, also useless because a biro doesn't write on wet paper. A pencil would have worked but I didn't have one. Weighing up my feelings about a cold wet bed against my mistrust of the Kurds here, I stopped overnight at a yaila. The women helped me to dry out my clothes on their dung-fuelled fire, and were as kind and hospitable as Kurds can be. Keyif was a bundle of energy, racing to and fro on his tether and roaring at the mares, he had no interest in food, water or sleep.

Dawn was misty, and when I went to collect Keyif he seemed to have no outline, just a grey blur in a grey fog. He was still prancing with energy, his mane streaming out and his nostrils steaming. A cold damp morning, I shivered uncomfortably and we got rather lost because mist shrouded the whole landscape; billowing and thinning, putting stark lines into soft focus. At our highest point I saw, looming blackly out of the opalescent blur, the tall prow-like shape of the Ark Rock. From this angle it certainly did look convincingly like a ship.

A shepherd I met said that the mist could stay for days. That was enough for me and I headed Keyif downhill. As we came down we reached the level where the clouds ended and beneath us was warm sunshine. Below that, the descent through lava spews grew continually hotter until around us was a volcanic bomb-field, scorching under a relentless sun.

I didn't mind about not reaching the summit. One cannot fail unless one sets out to succeed. Goals are like destinations, they don't always matter. Our journey was enough in itself.

The End of the World

Edmund Stump

Editors' note: Ed Stump is a professor of geology at Arizona State University and has spent ten seasons in the Antarctic. He has published dozens of scientific papers about the Transantarctic Mountains and written several books about geology, including The Roof at the Bottom of the World, The Ross Orogen of the Transantarctic Mountains, *and* Geology of Arizona. *Here he describes a 1987 trip to the Transantarctic Mountains.*

On December 19, 1929, six men mushed dogs across an endless tract of blue ice. Their destination had been the Transantarctic Mountains, a chain of rugged peaks deep within Antarctica where they radioed weather reports to Admiral Byrd during the South Pole's first flyover. Leader of the ground party and Byrd's second in command was geologist Lawrence M. Gould. The chief dog handler was 24-year-old Norman Vaughan, who would later have a peak named after him, and would return in 1995 at the age of 88 to climb it.

On that near-solstice day in 1929, the men were so intent on reaching their next landfall they failed to notice they were midway across the mouth of a massive outlet glacier—now known as Scott Glacier. When they finally made camp that night, they stood in awe of the sweeping walls and ragged peaks that lined the icy corridor.

Byrd returned four years later to continue exploring the Antarctic. In an epic journey of crevasses and wind, three members of his team—Quin Blackburn, Stuart Paine, and Richard Russell—sledged with dogs to Gould's endpoint, then traversed up Scott Glacier to its headreaches. Their goal was to chart the exposed sedimentary layers that cap the Transantarctic Mountains at Mount Weaver. There, the three climbed, surveyed, and collected 67 rock samples, including coal. From the summit of Mount Weaver they discovered Mount Howe, 30 miles to the south, the southernmost outcrop of rock on earth.

In 1969 and 1970 a New Zealand geological party of six used motor toboggans to traverse Scott Glacier, and bagged the first ascent of Mount Pulitzer, via the ice face on the northern side. An account of their sledge trip was published in the 1970 New Zealand *Alpine Journal*. As with Blackburn's 1937 account in *Geographical Review*, the Organ Pipe Peaks were featured in dramatic, stirring photos.

I knew the photos well when in 1971 I flew to Scott Glacier. Along with several other graduate students from Ohio State, I had lucked onto a helicopter-supported geological party working in the Transantarctic Mountains.

I had intended to drop out of school after the trip and travel, but when I finally returned to the world of green, warmth, and night, my unrelenting passion became that alien land. I continued my graduate studies at Ohio State, where I worked obstinately to put together another Antarctic trip.

Three times between 1977 and 1981, I returned to the Scott Glacier area to map and collect geological samples for the National Science Foundation. The NSF has strict policies about not supporting climbing or private expeditions, and for the scientific parties it does support, climbing for climbing's sake is taboo. My trips were driven by scientific research, but by necessity included mountaineering.

The guide for several of my Antarctic seasons was my brother Mugs. He started the 1970s as defensive halfback for Penn State, then spent a year in semi-pro ball getting his head kicked in before deciding to become a ski bum in the deep powder of Snowbird, Utah. At first, skiing was everything to him; summer was work to turn a coin. But the mountains and their crags caught hold, and soon Mugs was working in the winter and climbing in the Wasatch in the summer.

By the end of the 1970s, Mugs was a top alpinist, having climbed the Emperor Face on Mount Robson and the Super Couloir on Fitzroy. No one was more qualified to serve as field assistant to my 1980–81 Antarctic party, whose goal was to map the La Gorce Mountains in the southeast quadrant of Scott Glacier.

A ski-fitted Hercules C-130 dropped us near Ackerman Ridge. We completed our mapping, then traversed the east side of Scott Glacier to the Gothic Mountains, where we would collect granite samples from the flanks and summits of the peaks.

Protruding into Scott Glacier, Grizzly Peak is the granite watchtower to the Gothic Mountains. Phil Colbert, Mugs, and I tackled its south face, soloing a series of snow-choked cracks and chimneys to a gendarmed ridge and the summit.

On our last day of that season Mugs and I climbed the center spire of the Organ Pipes, a series of toothy towers within the Gothics. The route up the north side was an uncertain series of runnels, snowfields, and mixed terrain. Two pitches into the mixed climbing, the angle slacked to 60-degree snow, and we unroped. We then tacked back and forth, and just before the summit discovered a small, natural bridge that we crawled through. The summit of The Spectre, as we would call it, was a special one for Mugs and me, for we both knew that the climb of one of the world's most remote and beautiful peaks would not have been possible without each other—I needed Mugs for his climbing expertise, he needed me for the trip.

As kids Mugs and I had tramped the ridges of central Pennsylvania, and climbed the sheer and crumbling walls of Quigley's limestone quarry. But this season in the Antarctic was our first stretch together as adults. We took a hero shot on the summit for Mom and Dad.

As I lay in my bag that night I gazed across Scott Glacier to the towering walls of the Hays Mountains, over in the last quadrant of Scott Glacier, the one I had yet to study. That vista hung in my mind as the years passed and I did research in other parts of the Transantarctic Mountains. It hung there like the remembrance of a dream recalled so often you can no longer distinguish it from reality.

In 1987 that dream came true. I was back on the Scott Glacier with a New Zealander, Paul Fitzgerald, who was using fission-track dating to chronicle the Transantarctic uplift. Our mission was to collect samples from the highest summits. Mugs was there again, along with Lyle Dean, a second mountain guide.

From our first campsite east of the Medina Peaks, we climbed 20 or so small foothills, then traversed the snowy fringes of the Koerwitz Glacier, toward the dramatic northeast buttress of Mount Griffith. From there, a huge drift led us to the pass between Griffith and Mount Pulitzer. Beyond the pass we entered a stark, medieval-looking world that we named the Dragon's Lair. To the east was Mount Pulitzer (or The Dragon) and its craggy ridgeline. To the west was Mount Astor, at 12,175 feet the highest peak in the Hays Mountains. Flanking Mount Astor were Mount Vaughan (10,302 feet) and Mount Crockett (11,386 feet). Across Scott Glacier to the southeast we could see the Gothic Mountains.

Our plan was to try the northeast buttress of Griffith by following the snow on its right-hand slope, and then rappel the mixed face so, as Mugs said, "You scientists can collect your *spec-ee-mans*."

We woke to the sort of Antarctic silence where you hear the blood pulsing in your ears. Taking advantage of the settled conditions, we drove out for a serious day in the mountains. Caching one snowmobile at the base, we drove the other two up a thousand-foot ramp between a ridge and massive icefall. From there, we started the long slog up the ice.

About midway up the buttress the slope steepened to 50 degrees. We arrived at the top of the buttress in about five hours. The euphoria of exertion soon subsided, so we took a summit rock sample, rappelled two pitches, and downclimbed, picking up a 10-pound rock every 300 feet, collecting 16 samples on what we named the Fission Wall.

The weather was marginal for the next week, but the winds finally abated long enough for us to attempt Griffith's summit. The 4,000 feet to the top followed a route similar to the one on the Fission Wall: a long, smooth ice slope next to a rocky drop. The summit view from Mount Griffith was unsurpassed and told of earlier polar exploration. For the first time we were able to see west, into the intricate ridge systems of the lower Amundsen Glacier, and beyond to the blocky massifs of Mount Fridtjof Nansen and Mount Don Pedro Christophersen, between which Roald Amundsen had forged his way to the South Pole in 1911.

Our next objective was Heinous Peak, a satellite of Mount Crockett. Aerial photos showed huge walls and ridges of bare rock, but we weren't certain that there was a feasible route to the top, and back down. On the far side of Forbidden Valley, we found the key to the mountain, a couloir filled with blue ice that met an angling snow gully that terminated at the summit.

It was another five days before the wind dropped enough to attempt the climb, with 7,500 feet of relief, our longest of the season. We front-pointed most of the couloir, and as I exited onto a ramp of mercifully soft, 45-degree snow, I shook with exhaustion. The others had waited, then gotten cold, and started for the top. I trudged up alone, and was soon squinting into three smiling faces masked by sunglasses and hoar frost. I sat, scanned the crest through half-closed eyes, then paid the piper with 18 samples and returned to basecamp after 20 hours in the field.

After our climb of Crockett, we broke camp at the Dragon's Lair, snowmobiled south along the west side of Scott Glacier, and pitched camp at the foot of a rugged group of granite peaks north of the confluence of the Souchez and Scott Glaciers. After dinner, Mugs and I were out on the moraine behind camp, wondering as we had so often before why no one else was out in the cold, photographing the sastrugi and fractured ice, rapt in the patterns.

As Mugs glassed the north face of Mount Borcik, the highest peak of the group, we played the old themes of climber and geologist. Mugs saw routes, I saw rocks. The next day we followed an icy trough to a faulted cleft that led to mixed ground and Borcik's summit.

Our final climb was to be Mount Zanuck on the opposite side of Scott Glacier. But for several days, clouds hung less than 300 feet above camp. When the clouds did finally lift, Paul and I ran out and climbed a lesser peak, Altar Peak, to calibrate our altimeters. Weather held, however, so Paul and I loaded up on spaghetti and went out again to finish Zanuck. Mugs and Lyle, who had exhausted themselves reconnoitering the area, opted to rest in camp.

Moderate snow climbing and easy rock took us to within 70 feet of the summit. A light sprinkling of snow rose with us up the slope. We stashed our packs on the summit ridge and scrambled the short distance to the top. The south face of Zanuck dropped away in a sheer sweep. A fog bank on the lower Scott Glacier had crept into Sanctuary Glacier, engulfed camp, and crossed the saddle to Grizzly Peak. Beyond, spotted with cloud, Scott Glacier stretched to Mount Howe.

It was now more than 30 hours since Paul and I had slept, but my feeling of completion overrode that of exhaustion. I'd done the fourth and final quadrant, with closure in the Gothic Mountains. There was no place left on Scott Glacier I wanted to see, no dream left unfulfilled. I also felt a sense of loss, one that accompanies the attainment of a quest. There was a sudden lack of purpose where before there had been a goal. So, it was with mixed feelings that for the last time I bashed loose a sample, shouldered my pack, and carefully began the downclimb that would lead home.

ABOUT THE EDITORS

Cameron M. Burns is an award-winning writer, editor, and photographer based in Colorado. He has been writing about environmental, green architecture, energy, and sustainability issues since the late 1980s as a reporter/correspondent with various newspapers and as a contributing editor with numerous magazines. His essays, articles, op-eds, features, blogs, and other material on sustainability issues have been featured in publications and on websites around the globe. He is the editor of *The Essential Amory Lovins* and coauthor of *Building Without Borders*; *Writing, Etc.*; and *Contact: Mountain Climbing and Environmental Thinking*. He is also a prolific writer, photographer, and editor in the outdoors/adventure world. He wrote the first ice climbing guide to Colorado and coauthored the first guidebook to California fourteeners—and has authored, coauthored, and contributed to more than thirty books on climbing, the outdoors, and adventure. See cameronburns.com for more.

Kerry L. Burns grew up in Tasmania. As a geologist in the 1950s and 1960s, he explored the Tasmanian wilderness, the Australian outback, and the Cordillera Darwin in Tierra del Fuego in South America. His experiences in the coal industry of Australia and the United States led him to look for alternate sources of energy, and at Los Alamos National Laboratory he participated in the Hot Dry Rock geothermal projects at Fenton Hill, New Mexico, and Clear Lake, California. He is currently a geothermal energy consultant for projects in Australia, Europe, and North America.